3ds Max®
at a Glance

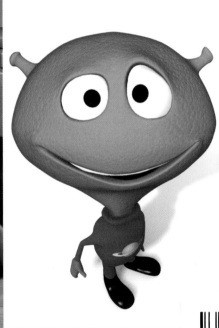

George Maestri

BICENTENNIAL
1807
WILEY
2007
BICENTENNIAL

Wiley Publishing, Inc.

Acquisitions Editor: Mariann Barsolo
Development Editor: Pete Gaughan
Technical Editor: Keith Reicher
Production Editor: Elizabeth Ginns Britten
Copy Editor: Sharon Wilkey
Production Manager: Tim Tate
Vice President and Executive Group Publisher: Richard Swadley
Vice President and Executive Publisher: Joseph B. Wikert
Vice President and Publisher: Neil Edde
Associate Project Editor: Laura Atkinson
Associate Producer: Kate Jenkins
Media Quality Assurance: Angie Denny
Book Designer: Mark Ong
Compositor: Denise Hom and Susan Riley, Side By Side Studios
Proofreader: Nancy Riddiough
Indexer: Nancy Guenther
Anniversary Logo Design: Richard Pacifico
Cover Designer: Ryan Sneed
Cover Image: George Maestri

Dear Reader,

Thank you for choosing *3ds Max at a Glance*. This book is part of a family of premium quality Sybex books, all written by outstanding authors who combine practical experience with a gift for teaching.

Sybex was founded in 1976. More than thirty years later, we're still committed to producing consistently exceptional books. With each of our titles we're working hard to set a new standard for the industry. From the paper we print on, to the authors we work with, our goal is to bring you the best books available.

I hope you see all that reflected in these pages. I'd be very interested to hear your comments and get your feedback on how we're doing. Feel free to let me know what you think about this or any other Sybex book by sending me an email at nedde@wiley.com, or if you think you've found a technical error in this book, please visit http://sybex.custhelp.com. Customer feedback is critical to our efforts at Sybex.

Best regards,

Neil Edde
Vice President and Publisher
Sybex, an Imprint of Wiley

Acknowledgments

Many thanks to my kids, friends, and family, and many, many thanks to everyone at Sybex who helped me with creating such a beautiful book.

About the Author

George Maestri has worked as a writer, director, and producer in both traditional and computer animation and has 15 years of animation experience at most of the major studios. Animation is his second career. His first job, at age 16, was programming computers. He earned a degree in computer science and soon was working in Silicon Valley on high-end computer graphics systems. Being an artist and a musician, George always had a creative streak, and he ultimately left the high-technology world to study art and animation.

After working on several independent films, George's first big break in animation was developing the pilot for *Rocko's Modern Life*, a Nickelodeon series that he also helped write. He since has also worked for Film Roman, Disney, Warner Brothers, MGM, Threshold Digital Research Labs, Curious Pictures, and Comedy Central, where he was one of the original producers of the hit series *South Park*. His characters "Karen and Kirby" have appeared on Kid's WB.

As an educator George has, among his many books, published several volumes of *Digital Character Animation*, which was created as the first computer animation book aimed at artists. George has taught at Otis College of Art, Nanyang Polytechnic in Singapore, University of California Santa Cruz, Dhima, and lynda.com.

George is the owner of Rubber Bug, a digital animation production facility. In addition to production work, Rubber Bug develops and packages original concepts for the broadcast and educational markets.

George resides in Los Angeles with his son and daughter and Alex, the wonder dog.

Contents at a Glance

Contents

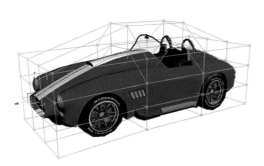

3   **Creating Textures   47**

4   Lighting   67

5   Rendering   87

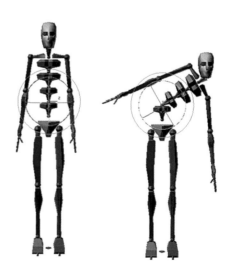

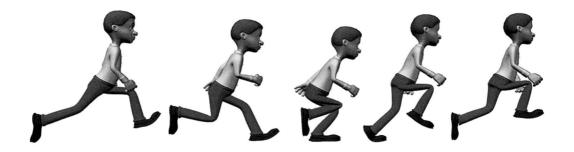

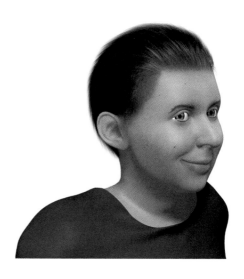

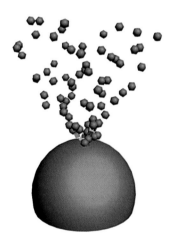

Introduction

Many years ago, I was a frustrated software engineer working in Silicon Valley. I was in a very technical field, which I enjoyed, but I also had a strong desire to exercise my artistic side. Writing code for Unix workstations just didn't satisfy that. I loved cartoons, so I decided to take the plunge and learn animation by taking some night courses at a local college. Even back then, when I was learning to draw animation a frame at a time, I found it to be a great balance of right- and left-brain activities. You could get a good creative right-brain rush by drawing lots and lots of pictures, but there were also the technical left-brain tasks of making those images move and bringing them to the screen.

As computers started to work their way into the animation world, I found that this creative/technical split became even more pronounced. People were either programmers or artists, but there were very few who were both. Soon packages such as 3ds Max came along that helped bridge that gap. 3ds Max is the perfect package for confused right/left-brain types such as me. 3ds Max can be as technical as you would ever want, yet it still allows an artist to easily create stunningly beautiful images.

For the artist, learning something as technical as 3ds Max can seem daunting, and for technical people, creating a beautiful image can be challenging. Hopefully, this book will bridge more of the gap by providing much of its information visually. By explaining this somewhat technical topic in a visual way that is easy to understand, this book will appeal to those who use 3ds Max.

This book is certainly not an encyclopedia of 3ds Max, but as its cover says, it shows you all the major features of 3ds Max "at a glance." Although the book is compact, we've tried to pack a lot of good information on 3ds Max into a small space. You should be able to flip open the book and see most of the pertinent information on a topic within a single set of pages. For those just learning 3ds Max, I have also added tutorials at the end of each chapter to give you hands-on coverage of some of the more-important tasks covered in the book. By reading through each chapter and working through the tutorials, *3ds Max at a Glance* can also be used as an introductory course for those learning 3ds Max.

Ideally, this book will appeal to those just getting started in 3ds Max as well as those with experience who need a handy reference. Whatever category you fall into, I hope you enjoy *3ds Max at a Glance*.

What's Inside

Here is a brief synopsis of what we will cover:

Chapter 1, Introduction to 3ds Max: This chapter gives you the basic road map so you know where things are in 3ds Max. You'll understand the basic interface, file management, and how to navigate within the package.

Chapter 2, Modeling: Modeling is the starting point for creating a 3D scene. Modeling is the digital equivalent of sculpting, and in this chapter you'll learn how to sculpt surfaces by using wireframes and patches instead of clay and stone.

Chapter 3, Creating Textures: 3ds Max's texture tools give you the freedom to color and shade your surfaces in any way desired. This chapter covers the creation of shaders and textures, as well as how to map those textures on a model.

Chapter 4, Lighting: This chapter covers the many methods for adding and manipulating light within the scene.

Chapter 5, Rendering: Rendering in 3ds Max can be done by using the program's own tools or the mental ray renderer. This chapter explains all the rendering features and effects for both renderers, including mental ray's global illumination and caustics tools.

Chapter 6, Character Deformations and Rigging: 3ds Max offers several tools for deforming meshes as well as rigging characters for animation. This chapter shows how to rig a character as well as explaining topics such as skeletons, deformers, and skinning.

Chapter 9, Animation: Animation is where you bring a scene to life. This chapter covers 3ds Max's animation tools, including the Curve Editor and Dope Sheet as well as the Motion panel.

Chapter 8, Character Studio: Character Studio has tools such as Biped that can be used to animate characters, create automatic walks and runs, and apply motion capture data.

Chapter 9, Special Effects: Special effects artists use 3ds Max's dynamics tools to accurately simulate reality. This chapter gives a good overview of particle systems and the forces that affect them as well as hard and soft body dynamics.

Chapter 10, Hair and Cloth: 3ds Max has tools to create realistic hair, fur, and cloth. This chapter goes over the basics of these tools and shows you how to style a great virtual hairdo and sew a stylish virtual shirt.

Note

The companion CD contains all the images and source files used in the step-by-step tutorials throughout the book. Use these to follow along with the instructions as you try out the methods in each chapter. See the appendix for details on accessing the CD contents.

How to Contact the Author

I'd love to hear your feedback to this book. You can reach me through my company's website, www.rubberbug.com.

Note: Sybex strives to keep you supplied with the latest tools and information you need for your work. Please check www.sybex.com for additional content and updates that supplement this book and CD.

Introduction to 3ds Max

3ds Max is a powerful 3D modeling, animation, effects, and rendering solution that has been used in everything from video games to feature films. 3ds Max has a wealth of features that can tackle almost any sort of project and generate incredibly realistic or highly stylized images.

3ds Max's large feature set may seem daunting to the newcomer, but the software has a consistent and easy-to-use interface, and this chapter introduces that interface. Once you have your feet wet, you can move on to the other areas of 3ds Max, covered in greater depth in subsequent chapters. By learning the package a little bit at a time, you'll discover the true power of 3ds Max.

Understanding the 3ds Max Interface

Understanding the 3ds Max interface is the foundation of everything you'll do within the software, including modeling objects, creating textures, animating, and final rendering.

Menu bar Contains text-driven menus for all of the major features.

Toolbar Provides graphic representations of the most important and commonly used features, such as undoing, object linking, selecting, transforming, texturing, and rendering, among others.

Command panel Contains six tabbed panels (Create, Modify, Hierarchy, Motion, Display, Utilities) that contain rollouts to control just about every aspect of the scene.

Viewports Used mainly to view your 3D scenes through camera or perspective views. Viewports can also contain data about the scene, such as animation curves or schematics of the scene.

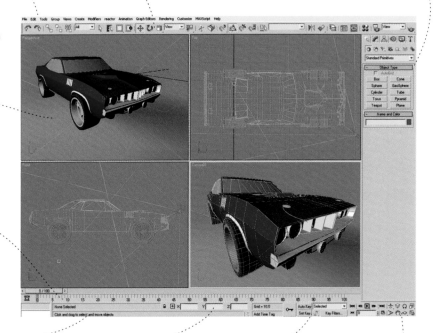

Timeline Lets you scrub through the scene and manipulate keyframes.

Help line Provides a short description of the tools and how to use them.

Transforms Numeric values for each of the transforms (Move, Rotate, Scale) can be viewed or changed.

Keyframe tools A collection of tools to create and manage keyframes.

Navigation tools Tools used to navigate within viewports.

Toolbar

The **toolbar** menu contains graphic representations of many major features of 3ds Max. The menu can be floated by left-clicking and dragging the double vertical line on the far left of the menu.

Undo/Redo Multiple undos are possible. The maximum can be set in the Customize → Preferences menu.

Selection filter Allows you to isolate the objects selected to specific types, such as geometry, lights, cameras, and so forth.

Select By Name Brings up a floating menu, where objects can be selected by name.

Transform tools Tools to move, rotate, and scale objects.

Select And Manipulate Tool used to manipulate special parameters in an object.

Selection Sets Allows the creation of custom selection sets. Select objects and then type in a name to create a set.

Curve Editor Edits animation curves in a scene.

Material Editor Creates a floating window used to create, edit, and modify materials.

Linking Tools to link objects in hierarchies, break those links, and link objects to space warps.

Selection Region Pulling down this menu allows you to change the way objects are selected (Rectangular, Circular, Lasso, and Paint Region)

Snap tools Tools used to accurately snap objects while transforming them.

Schematic View Creates a floating Schematic View window.

Select Objects Activates the Select tool used to select objects.

Coordinate System Defines which coordinate system (Local, View, Screen, Parent, World) is used to transform objects.

Layer Manager Manages the layers in a 3ds Max scene.

Rendering tools Tools used for rendering the scene and controlling rendering options.

Command Panel

The **Command panel** is located to the right of the main viewports, along the right edge of the interface. This is one of the most used sections of the 3ds Max interface and contains six tabbed panels: Create, Modify, Hierarchy, Motion, Display, and Utilities.

Modify Contains modifiers that can be applied to objects to control a myriad of tasks, such as modeling, animation, texturing, and more

Hierarchy Contains tools for managing links in a hierarchy, joints, and inverse kinematics

Motion Contains tools for creating and modifying animation and trajectories as well as applying animation controllers

Display Contains tools that modify the way objects are displayed, along with tools to hide, unhide, and freeze objects

Create Contains tools for creating objects such as geometry, cameras, lights, and more

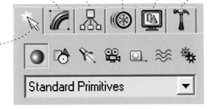

Utilities Contains miscellaneous utility programs and plug-ins to help manage the scene and objects within the scene

Viewports

Viewports are where most of the work is done within 3ds Max. Viewports hold views of your scene as well as other types of windows that display information about your scene. There are two types of scene views within 3ds Max: perspective and orthographic.

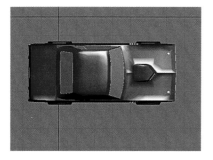  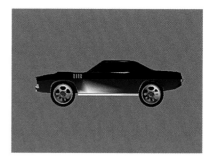

Orthographic views, such as top, left, and front allow only Pan and Zoom.

Perspective views can also be rotated in 3D space.

 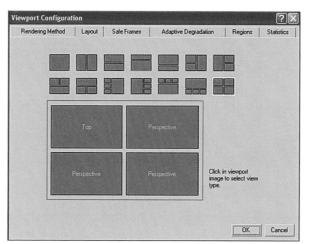

The Viewport Configuration menu enables you to change the arrangement of the viewports as well as decide the way those viewports will be rendered.

Right-click over the title of the viewport to bring up the Views menu. This enables you to change the type of view as well as the shading method. There are also options to display grids and safe frames, as well as configure the viewport.

Shading

Each viewport can have its own type of **shading**, for viewing different parts of the scene in different ways. When you are modeling, you may choose to work in wireframe mode, and when rendering, you may choose one of the shaded modes. The quality of the shading depends on the graphics card as well as the graphics mode. Direct3D drivers are faster and will show more-realistic textures and transparencies, whereas OpenGL drivers are faster for deforming meshes, such as in character animation.

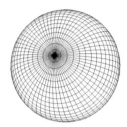

Wireframe shows a basic outline of the object.

Smooth shows the object rendered.

Wireframe On Shaded shows the wireframe superimposed on a shaded object.

Facets shows the model without smoothing, making the polygonal edges visible.

Flat eliminates shading for a more-2D look.

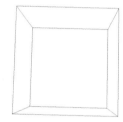

Bounding Box creates a box around the object. Bounding Box is great for navigating complex scenes that update slowly in the more-detailed modes.

Navigation

Navigation in 3ds Max can be accomplished by using the mouse or by using the navigation bar at the bottom-right corner of the screen. Mouse navigation is accomplished by using the middle button along with the keyboard.

Middle-click and drag to pan the viewport.

Roll the middle button to zoom. If the mouse does not have a rolling middle button, press Ctrl+Alt while pressing the middle button to zoom.

Hold down the Ctrl key while pressing the middle button to rotate around the scene.

The navigation bar at the bottom-right corner of the screen contains additional navigation tools.

Zoom Zooms the active viewport

Zoom All Zooms all viewports

Frame Frames the selected object(s) in the viewport

Frame All Frames the selected object(s) in all viewports

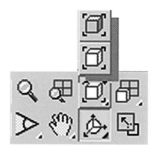

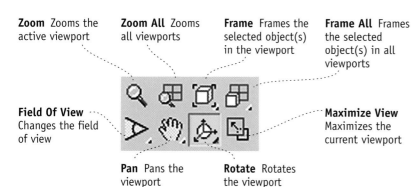

Field Of View Changes the field of view

Maximize View Maximizes the current viewport

Clicking the Frame, Frame All, and Rotate icons brings up a selection menu. Gray icons act on the entire scene, and white icons act on the selected object.

Pan Pans the viewport

Rotate Rotates the viewport

Quadmenus

Quadmenus are a set of context-sensitive menus that activate at the cursor when you right-click in any viewport. Up to four menus appear and contain the most commonly used commands for the particular situation. If you're modeling, for example, modeling commands will appear.

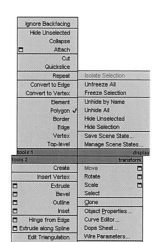

In a quadmenu, Display and Transform tools are in the right quadrants, while context-sensitive tools are on the left.

Selecting Objects

3ds Max has a wide variety of object types, such as geometry, lights, cameras, and bones, among others. 3ds Max can select objects individually, by group, and by name.

Objects can be selected individually or in groups by using the mouse. When left-clicking an object selects it, left-clicking and dragging selects a region. Holding down the Ctrl key while selecting adds to a selection, and holding down the Alt key removes from the selection.

Select Selects the object by using the mouse.

Select By Name Brings up the Select By Name floating menu.

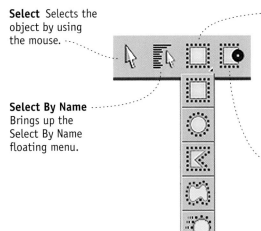

Selection Region Clicking and holding this icon enables you to change the way objects are selected: rectangular, circular, polygonal lasso, lasso, and paint.

Window/Crossing This determines whether objects need to be entirely within the selection region to be selected.

Name Type-In Typing in a name or partial name selects all objects that match.

List The objects in the scene listed by name.

Subtrees/ Dependents Organizes the list by hierarchies or dependencies.

List Types Displays or hides objects in the list according to type.

Selection Set Selects a predefined selection set.

Sort Sorts the list by object name, type, color, or size.

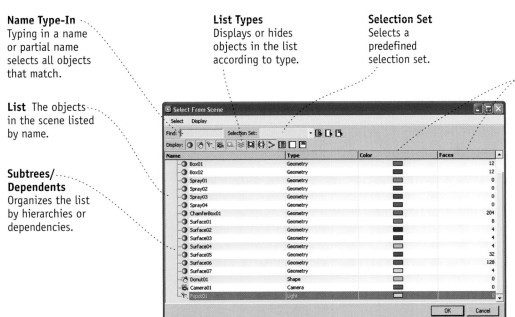

The Select From Scene floating menu

Groups of selected objects can be given names so they can be reselected later. This is done by using the Selection Sets pull-down menu on the main toolbar. To create a set, simply type the name of the set and hit Enter. This places the set in the pull-down menu, where it can be recalled later. Sets can be edited by left-clicking the icon to the left of the pull-down.

Transforming Objects

Selected objects can be moved, rotated, and scaled. These transforms can be accessed by using the icons on the main toolbar or by pressing the hot keys W (Move), E (Rotate), and R (Scale).

Each transform uses a color-coded gizmo. Red transforms along the X-axis, green along the Y-axis, and blue along the Z-axis. Clicking and dragging in the center of the gizmo transforms the object on all available axes, while clicking in the box connecting two axes transforms on only those two axes.

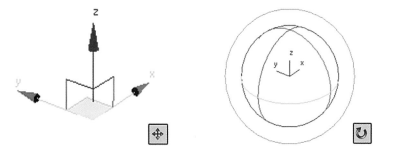

Move gizmo   Rotate gizmo   Scale gizmo

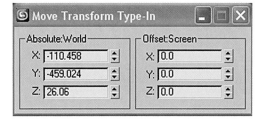

Right-clicking the Move, Rotate, or Scale icon brings up a floating menu that accepts numeric input.

Coordinate Systems

Transformations can take place along a number of user-selectable XYZ coordinate systems. These change how the transform gizmo is oriented relative to the object. 3ds Max has several types of coordinate systems, including View, Screen, World, and Parent.

Pivots

The **pivot** is the center of each object's coordinate system, which is particularly important when rotating an object, because the object will rotate around the pivot. Pivots are managed in the Command panel under the Pivot panel of the Hierarchy tab.

When the pivot is placed outside the wheel, the wheel rotates around its edge.

When the pivot is in the center of the wheel, it rotates around the axle.

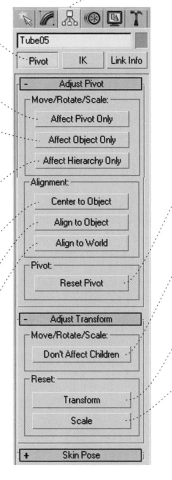

Hierarchy tab The Pivot panel is located under the Hierarchy tab.

Pivot panel This panel contains tools to adjust an object's pivot.

Affect Pivot Only Allows you to move the position of the pivot.

Affect Object Only Allows you to move the object while the pivot remains stationary.

Affect Hierarchy Only Applies the rotation or scale to the hierarchy by rotating or scaling the position of the pivot point without rotating or scaling the pivot point itself.

Center To Object Moves the pivot to the center of its object.

Align To Object Rotates the pivot to align with the object's transformation axis.

Align To World Rotates the pivot to align with the world axis.

Reset Pivot Resets the pivot to when the object was first created.

Don't Affect Children Moves the pivot without affecting the position of child objects in the hierarchy.

Reset Transform Resets the transform to zero.

Reset Scale Resets the scale of the object to 100 percent.

Snapping

The **Object Snapping tools** are good for snapping objects to precise positions. When you are moving objects, these tools let you snap objects to grids, other objects, or parts of other objects. Rotations can be snapped so the object rotates in specific increments. There are three snap modes:

 2D snap snaps only in 2D space along grids; the vertical dimension is ignored.

 2D snap snaps in 2D space along grids, but maintains the vertical dimension. The effect is like holding up a sheet of glass and drawing the outline of an object on it.

 This is the default. The cursor snaps directly to any geometry in 3D space.

Vertex Snaps to a polygonal, mesh, or patch vertex

Endpoint Snaps to the end points of edges on meshes or spline vertices

Midpoint Snaps to the middle of edges on meshes and spline segments

Edge/Segment Snaps to a polygonal or mesh edge or a spline segment

Face Snaps anywhere on the surface of a face

Frozen Snaps to frozen objects

Pivot Snaps to the pivot point of an object

Axis Constraints Brings up the axis constraints toolbar, which limits motion along specified axes

Grid Points Snaps to grid intersections

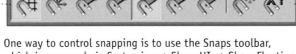

One way to control snapping is to use the Snaps toolbar, which is accessed via Customize → Show UI → Show Floating Toolbars.

Right-clicking the snaps icon brings up the Grid And Snap Settings menu. This floating menu offers more options and precise control over snapping.

Managing Objects

3ds Max has a number of tools that allow you to manage the display and behavior of objects within the scene. Objects can be organized by type, color, and name. Objects can also be hidden or frozen. This helps to organize scenes and eliminate clutter.

Hiding and Freezing Objects

3ds Max has the capability to hide objects from view, or to freeze them so that they can be viewed but not selected. If you're working with one set of objects, for example, you can hide or freeze other objects in the scene to make it easier to select and manipulate the desired objects. Selected objects can be hidden and/or frozen by using the quadmenu or the Display panel.

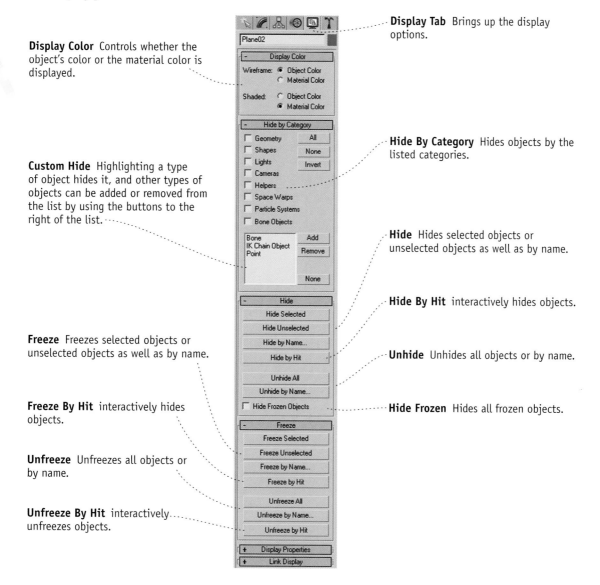

Display Tab Brings up the display options.

Display Color Controls whether the object's color or the material color is displayed.

Hide By Category Hides objects by the listed categories.

Custom Hide Highlighting a type of object hides it, and other types of objects can be added or removed from the list by using the buttons to the right of the list.

Hide Hides selected objects or unselected objects as well as by name.

Hide By Hit interactively hides objects.

Freeze Freezes selected objects or unselected objects as well as by name.

Unhide Unhides all objects or by name.

Freeze By Hit interactively hides objects.

Hide Frozen Hides all frozen objects.

Unfreeze Unfreezes all objects or by name.

Unfreeze By Hit interactively unfreezes objects.

Using Layers

Another way to manage objects is to separate them into layers by using the Layer Manager, which is accessed through the main toolbar. A **layer** is simply a collection of objects. Each layer has a unique name, and layers can be hidden or frozen. Layers can also be used for such tasks as rendering.

Create Layer Creates a new layer with the selected objects.

Add To Layer Adds selected objects to the active layer.

Hide All Hides all layers.

Freeze All Freezes all layers.

Hide Hides all objects in the layer.

Freeze Freezes all objects in the layer.

Layers A list of the current layers.

Active Layer The active layer is indicated by a check mark. Left-clicking a layer activates it.

Expand/Contract Click this icon to display the objects in the layer.

Render Turns rendering on/off for the current layer.

Color Changes the color of objects in the layer.

Radiosity Turns radiosity (a rendering parameter) on/off for the layer.

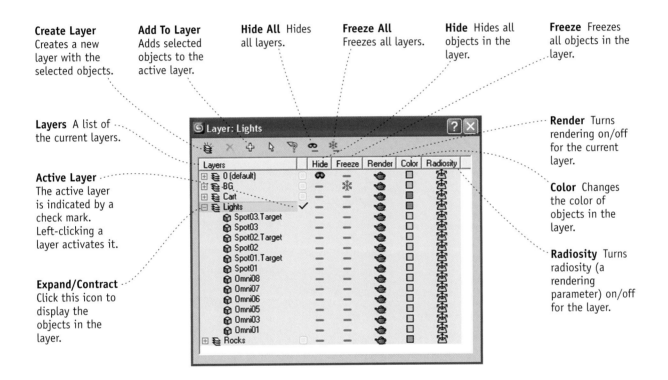

A complex scene such as this can be made easier to work with by hiding and freezing objects or separating the objects into layers.

Using Groups

3ds Max can also combine objects into groups by using the Group menu on the main menu. Once grouped, objects appear as a single object in your scene. You can click any object in the group to select the group object, and then transform or modify it however you choose. Groups can be nested, so you can group objects, and then group again with another set of groups or objects.

Group Combines selected objects or groups into a new group

Ungroup Removes the selected group, releasing the objects or groups

Open Opens the group, allowing you to transform or modify individual objects within the group

Close Closes an open group

Attach Attaches an object to an existing group

Detach Detaches an object from an existing group

Explode Ungroups all objects in a group, regardless of the number of nested groups

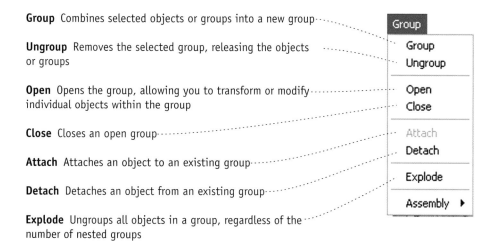

Linking Objects into Hierarchies

3ds Max can connect objects together in a hierarchy so that an object can parent other objects. Moving the parent object also moves the children. Hierarchies are very useful in animation because they can attach objects to one another, so when one object moves, the rest follow. Linking is done by using the Select And Link tool on the main toolbar. Select the object or objects to be linked, and drag the link to the desired parent.

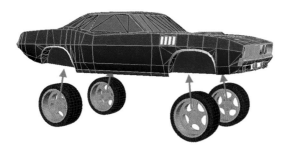

Using Select And Link, the wheels of this car are attached to the body as children in a hierarchy.

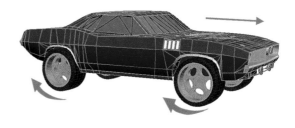

This allows the wheels to follow the body as it transforms, but also move and rotate around their own individual axes.

Hierarchy tab The Pivot panel is located under the Hierarchy tab.

Locks Selecting one of these check boxes will lock an object's motion along the specified axis.

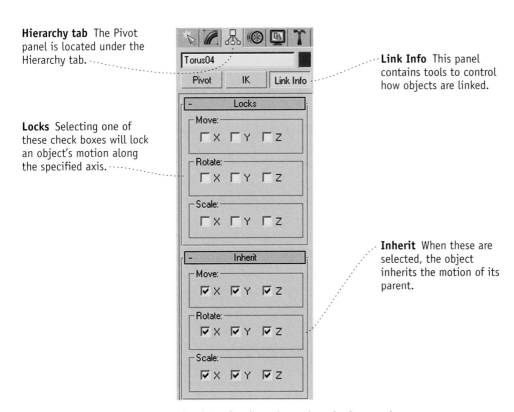

Link Info This panel contains tools to control how objects are linked.

Inherit When these are selected, the object inherits the motion of its parent.

The Link Info rollout, located on the Command panel, controls how objects link to each other and inherit those links.

Scene Explorer

Scene Explorer is a new feature in 3ds Max 2008. It presents a comprehensive view of all the objects in a scene. Objects can be sorted, filtered, and selected from within Scene Explorer. Changes can also be made to individual objects or groups of objects. Scene Explorer is very helpful for large scenes with many objects. Scene Explorer allows you to create custom views for different types of objects, so you could have a view to display just lights and lighting parameters, for example.

View Selects a custom Scene Explorer view.

Selection Set A pulldown that shows 3ds Max selection sets.

Select All Selects all objects in a scene.

Select None Deselects selected objects.

Select Invert Inverts the current selection.

Sync Selection Syncs the selection to the selection in the viewport.

Find Allows you to search the scene for objects the meet certain criteria.

Display Filters Turns objects on or off depending on type.

Object List A list of objects in the scene. Objects are listed hierarchically.

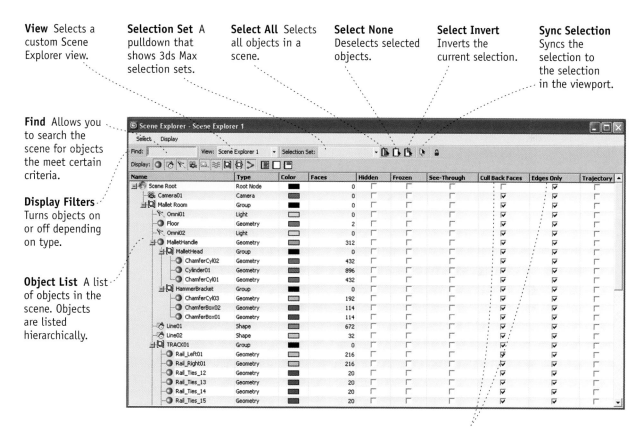

Object Parameters These columns can be customized to display a wide range of parameters. These allow for parameters to be changed to a selection of objects.

Customizing the Interface

Scene Explorer can be customized in several ways. The object filters determine the type of objects displayed, such as lights, cameras, geometry, bones, etc. The columns associated with each object can also be customized using the Column Chooser. Once a view has been customized, it can be saved by typing a name into the View box.

Filters Selecting just the light icon will display only lights.

View Typing a name here saves the view for later recall

Columns Click and drag a column to delete it. New columns can be added using the Column Chooser, which is accessed by right clicking over a column.

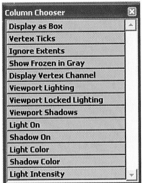

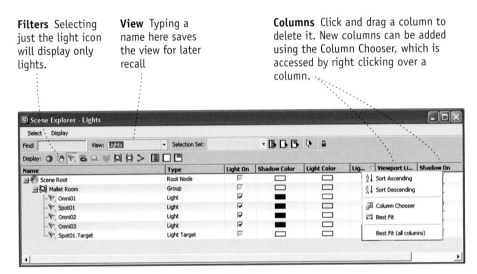

A custom Scene Explorer view to work with lighting.

The Column Chooser displays a list of parameters that can be placed in columns of a Scene Explorer View. Click and drag to place a new column into a view.

Using Scene Explorer

Scene Explorer can be used to select objects as well as change their parameters. Object can be selected by clicking, by using selection sets, or by using the Find utility. Selected objects appear in the 3ds Max scene. You can also change parameters for selected objects by adjusting the parameters listed in the columns.

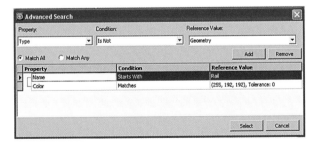

The Find utility allows you to search the scene for objects which meet specific critreria.

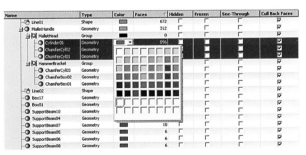

Clicking over a column for selected objects allows you to change the parameters for those objects. In this case, the color of the highlighted objects is being changed.

Modeling

Modeling is where most work starts in 3ds Max. Models represent the objects in your scene and can be anything from the objects composing a set to the characters that populate the set. Modeling is very close to sculpting, and like a good sculptor, a good modeler needs to have a good sense of form and volume.

Whereas a sculptor works with clay, stone, or some other physical material, a modeler works virtually with wireframes and geometry. 3ds Max provides a wealth of tools to shape and sculpt geometry into whatever shape you desire.

17

Understanding Geometry Types

3ds Max has several ways to represent geometry: meshes, polys, patches, and NURBS. Each type of geometry has its own way of representing a model, and each has its own benefits. Objects can be converted from one type to another, but ultimately, each type of model resolves to triangular polygons when the model is rendered.

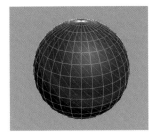 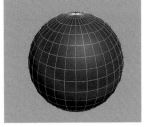  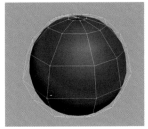

Editable mesh is a polygon-based object that uses triangular polygons. Editable meshes are useful for creating simple, low-polygonal objects or control meshes for subdivision surfaces. You can convert a NURBS or patch surface to an editable mesh. Editable meshes require little memory and are a natural method of modeling with polygonal objects.

Editable poly is a type of deformable object. An editable poly is a polygonal mesh; that is, unlike an editable mesh, it can use more than three-sided polygons. Editable polys are useful in that they avoid invisible edges and have a more-robust set of editing tools. You can convert NURBS surfaces, editable meshes, splines, primitives, and patch surfaces to editable polys.

Editable patch objects are useful for creating smooth surfaces, and provide very detailed controls for manipulating complex geometry. Unlike a polygonal object, a patch has curvature controls on each vertex to adjust the curvature of the surface.

NURBS modeling is exceptionally good at creating smooth, splined surfaces by using a minimum of points. NURBS is an acronym for non-uniform rational B-spline, the type of spline that defines a NURBS surface.

Creating Geometry

Geometry in 3ds Max is created by using either the Create menu on the main menu or the Geometry tab of the Create panel. This tab has a pull-down menu from which you can select different categories of objects to create. Most objects created are known as **parametric objects**. In other words, they use parameters to define the shape and form of the object. Only when an object is edited by using a modifier or modeling tool does it actually become a specific type of geometry.

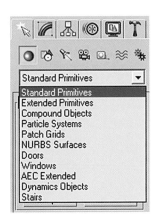

The Geometry tab of the Create panel has a pull-down menu from which you can access the different categories of objects.

The Create menu on the main menu bar also contains the same objects.

Basic Primitives

The **basic primitives** are basic shapes, such as spheres, boxes, and cylinders. Each shape has its own controls to define the size of the object and amount of detail, as well as other parameters unique to the type of object.

Box A box with definable detail. It is created by clicking on a viewport and dragging to define the base, and then dragging again to define the height.

Sphere A sphere shape with the geometry represented as latitudinal and longitudinal lines. A sphere is created by clicking in a viewport and dragging to the desired size.

Teapot This object is the standard Utah teapot. Click and drag to set the size.

Cone A cone is created by clicking on a viewport and dragging to define the base, and then dragging again to define the height.

Cylinder A cylinder is created by clicking on a viewport and dragging to define the base, and then dragging again to define the height.

Torus A doughnut shape. Created by clicking on the viewport to define the first radius and then dragging again for the second radius.

GeoSphere A spherical shape with the detail oriented in a geodesic pattern. This creates a smoother edge with less detail.

Tube A tube shape. Created by clicking and dragging to create the outer diameter, dragging again to create the inner diameter, and dragging a third time to define the length.

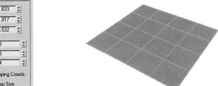

Pyramid A four-sided pyramid. Created by clicking on a viewport and dragging to define the base, and then dragging again to define the height.

Plane A flat plane. Created by clicking on a viewport and dragging to define the outer edges.

Extended Primitives

Extended primitives are of more-complex shapes. Sometimes these shapes will be closer to the form you need and can make good starting points for further modeling.

Hedra A polyhedral shape. Can be a tetrahedron, octahedron, dodecahedron, as well as a star shape.

Chamfer box A box with user-definable chamfers to round off the edges.

Oil tank A cylindrical shape with hemispherical caps on the ends.

Gengon A cylindrical shape with user-defined fillets between the major sections.

RingWave An object used in special effects to simulate shock waves.

Spindle A cylindrical shape with cone-shaped caps on the ends.

Prism A triangular prism.

Torus knot A shape with a complex knotted structure.

Chamfer cylinder A cylinder with user-definable chamfers to round off the edges.

Capsule A cylindrical shape with spherical end caps.

C-Ext An extruded object that resembles a C or a U shape.

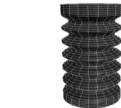

L-Ext An extruded object that resembles an L shape. Useful for creating walls.

Hose A user-definable hose.

Architectural Primitives

3ds Max has a wealth of **architectural primitives**. These can be anything from doors and windows to staircases to foliage. Mostly these are used by architects, but they can also be used in animation for sets and backgrounds.

Using Modifiers

After geometry is created, it can be further shaped by using modifiers. Modifiers are found under the Modifiers menu or in the in the Modifier List pull-down of the Modify panel. Modifiers can be used on the entire object or just parts of the object. They can also be combined by using the modifier stack to create more-complex shapes.

Parametric Deformers

Parametric deformers rely on user-defined parameters to change the shape of an object. This means you can change their values after they're applied and also animate them. Here are a few of the more commonly used deformers:

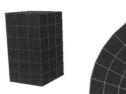 

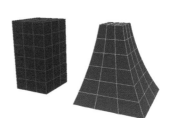 

Bend Bends the geometry around a user-definable axis

Taper Tapers an object with a user-definable curvature

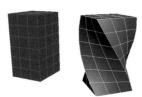 

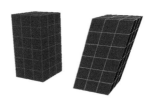

Twist Applies a screw-like twist to the object

Skew Skews the object in a user-defined direction

  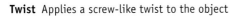

   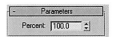

Relax Softens the hard edges of an object

Spherify Deforms the object to a spherical shape

Free-Form Deformation (FFD) Modifiers

Free-form deformation (FFD) is a class of modifiers that create a lattice of control points around an object. Manipulating the points of the lattice deforms the object. FFDs are used a lot as modeling tools, but they can also be animated, making them a good choice for animating anthropomorphic objects and creating special effects. 3ds Max has two main types of FFDs: box shaped and cylinder shaped. After an FFD is applied, it can be modified by accessing the Control Points sub-object within the modifier.

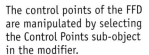

The control points of the FFD are manipulated by selecting the Control Points sub-object in the modifier.

A 4 × 4 × 4 FFD is applied to this car (left); modifying the FFD (right) reshapes the model.

Adjusting Modifiers

Modifiers can be stacked in the Modify panel to create complex effects. Changes to one modifier will flow through the stack, giving you a wide degree of control over the modifications to an object. Modifiers can be rearranged simply by clicking and dragging.

You can collapse all or part of the modifier stack. This locks in the changes and makes for a simpler object. Having a lot of modifiers on an object can take up a lot of system overhead, so collapsing the stack when an object is finished will make the scene update more quickly.

A Twist modifier is added to this box.

A Bend modifier is then added on top of the twist.

By changing the Twist modifier, you can affect the twist of the object within the bend.

Each modifier has a lightbulb icon next to it. Toggling the bulb icon off removes the effect.

Pin Modifier Keeps the modifier highlighted regardless of selection.

Show End Result Shows the result of the entire stack.

Each modifier shows up in the modifier stack in the order it was applied.

Modifiers can have sub-objects, which control different aspects of the modifier.

Configure Modifier Sets Allows you to select and configure sets of modifiers.

Remove Modifier Removes the selected modifier from the stack.

Using Splines

In 3ds Max, a **spline** is a Bezier-based line that defines a closed or open shape. Splines are typically used as building blocks to create other objects within 3ds Max, but they can also be rendered to create cylindrically shaped objects. Splines can also be used as animation paths or to control inverse kinematic (IK) chains.

Splines are created by using the Shapes tab of the Create panel. You can draw free-form lines or create a number of predefined shapes, such as circles, rectangles, helixes, and text.

Drawing Lines

The Line object under the Create panel will allow you to draw a line in a viewport. Lines are drawn by clicking in the viewport to lay down the vertices. Clicking the viewport creates the type of vertex defined under Initial Type, while clicking and dragging creates the type of vertex defined under Drag Type. This allows you to shape the line as it is drawn, reducing the amount of editing.

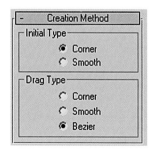

The Line object Create panel

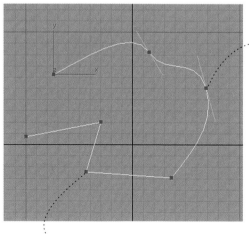

Clicking creates the ïinitial" type of vertex.

Clicking and dragging creates the "drag" type of vertex.

Editing Splines

Splines created by using the Line object have editing tools built in. Splines created by using any of the parametric tools such as Circle, Helix, or Text can be edited by applying an Edit Spline modifier to the stack. Splines have three classes of sub-objects: vertex, segment, and spline. **Vertices** are the points that define the line, **segments** are the portion of the spline between two vertices, and a **spline** is the entire line. A Spline object is not limited to a single line. A vertex on a spline can be one of four types:

Corner The line comes to a straight corner at the vertex.

Bezier corner The vertex has Bezier handles that are unlocked to create a corner.

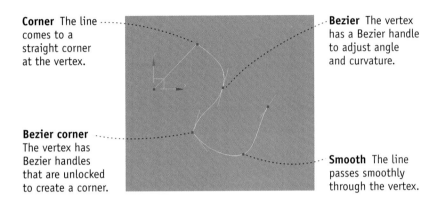

Bezier The vertex has a Bezier handle to adjust angle and curvature.

Smooth The line passes smoothly through the vertex.

Editing a spline is as simple as selecting the desired sub-objects and moving, rotating, or scaling them. Selections can be controlled by using the Selection rollout.

Selects vertices

Allows you to name your current selection for later recall

Allows you to manipulate multiple tangents at a time

Toggles on vertex numbering

Selects segments

Selects splines

Selects vertices, segments, or splines within a physical distance

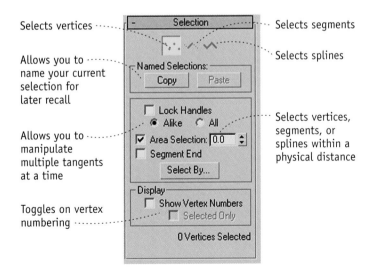

Besides manipulating the geometry itself, detail can be added to splines, and splines can be connected by using the tools located under the Geometry tab.

Right-clicking while editing a spline brings up a quad-menu, which gives you options to change the type of vertex, along with many other editing options.

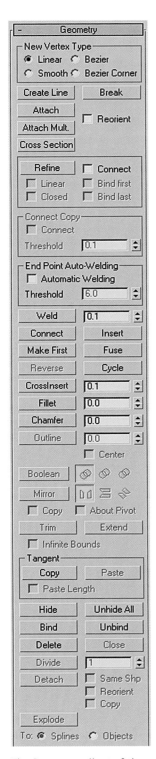

The Geometry rollout of the Edit Spline modifier is where most editing functions are located.

Attach Attaches another spline object to the current spline

Weld Welds two end points together to connect two splines as one

Connect Connects two end points together by using a segment

Insert Inserts a new vertex by clicking on a spline

Fillet Creates a rounded corner on a spline

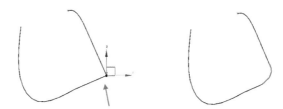

Chamfer Creates an angular corner on a spline

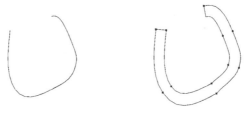

Outline Creates an outline for the selected spline

Rendering Splines

Any spline can be rendered, either in the viewport, renderer, or both. Splines are rendered as cylindrical shapes, and rendered splines can be an easy way to model all types of objects.

The Rendering rollout for Spline objects determines how the spline will be rendered.

This scene uses a Spline object for the railroad track. When the scene is rendered, the spline is rendered as rails.

Creating Geometry with Splines

The most common use of splines is as building blocks for other types of geometry. Because splines are curved shapes, they're excellent for creating smooth, organic surfaces. 3ds Max provides a number of tools to create objects by using splines.

Lathe The Lathe modifier revolves the spline around a user-defined axis to create a surface.

Extrude The Extrude modifier adds depth to a spline. It can be configured with caps on or off.

Sweep Sweep uses the spline as a path to sweep a user-defined shape, which can be selected from a pull-down list.

Loft Found under the Geometry/Compound Objects tab, Loft takes two separate splines and uses one for an extrusion, the other for the path. The shape can be further modified by using a deformation graph found under the Deformations rollout.

Surface The Surface modifier takes a "cage" made of splines and uses it as the basis to create a smooth surface. The cage is constructed by drawing multiple splines and snapping their vertices together at the intersection points.

Polygonal Modeling

Polygonal modeling is the most common form of modeling used in 3ds Max and is one of the more-intuitive ways to model. Polygonal models are easy to construct and have no topology limitations.

The downside to polygonal surfaces is that they are not resolution independent. Low-resolution polygonal models tend to animate quickly and are used extensively in games, but their lack of detail makes them undesirable for high-resolution rendering, such as for film or video. To overcome this limitation, 3ds Max has several subdivision surface modifiers that allow a low-res model to be smoothed automatically at render time so that artists can get the best of both worlds.

In 3ds Max, almost any type of object can be edited as a polygonal object. Adding an Edit Poly or Edit Mesh modifier to the stack will turn the object into a polygonal object. You can also right-click over the stack and collapse an object to a poly or mesh.

Polygonal Components

Polygonal surfaces have four major components: vertices, edges, faces, and elements. Editable mesh objects also have a triangular face sub-object, while editable poly objects have a border sub-object. To select one of these components, highlight an icon in the Selection rollout, select the sub-object in the modifier stack, or right-click over the surface to open a quadmenu, where the sub-object can be selected. The types of polygonal components are:

A vertex represents a single point in space; vertices are the building blocks of all polygonal objects.

An edge connects two vertices, forming a line. Edges also connect the sides of polygons or faces.

A border, in an editable poly object, is a connected loop of edges on the open border of an object.

A face, in an editable mesh, is a triangular plane.

A polygon, in a poly object, is a face that defines a plane; in an editable mesh, a polygon is a face composed of multiple triangles.

An element is a polygon that is not attached to a polygonal object.

Polygonal objects can be edited by using either the Edit Mesh or Edit Poly modifier. Objects can also be collapsed to editable mesh or editable poly objects. The big difference with editable mesh and editable poly is that poly objects can have polygons with any number of sides, whereas mesh objects are based in triangles. The Edit Poly modifier also has additional selection and editing tools, plus the ability to perform paint deformations and create subdivision surfaces. The editable mesh object is the simplest of the polygonal object types, and is used when precise control over the polygons is needed, such as when creating low-poly models for games. For most applications, editable poly is the preferred geometry because it imposes fewer limitations on the modeler and has a more robust set of tools.

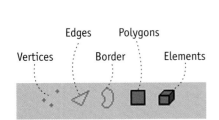

Editable Poly selection icons

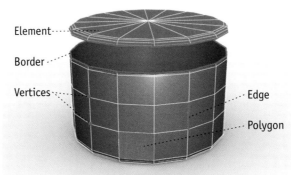

Editable Poly sub-objects

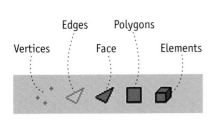

Editable Mesh selection icons

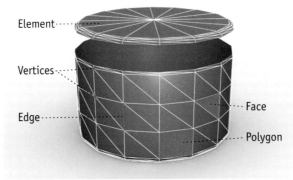

Editable Mesh sub-objects

Edit Poly Modifier

The Edit Poly modifier converts an object into an editable poly object. This modifier allows you to reshape the object and to add or subtract detail. In addition, the modifier has controls that aid in texturing an object as well as paint deformation and animation tools.

Left: A ring of edges. Right: A loop of edges.

Selecting Components

To select components in an object, highlight the sub-object type (vertex, edge, border, poly, element) in the Selection rollout or in the stack. After the type is highlighted, you can select the objects by using the standard selection tools.

Uses the active selection in the modifier below the current modifier.

Allows you to select a sub-object only by selecting a vertex that it uses

Does not select sub-objects that are facing away in the active viewport

Selects a ring of edges

Gets the active selection in the modifier below the current modifier

Selects a loop of edges

Determines what type of sub-object is active

Shrinks or grows a selection by one vertex, edge, or polygon

When SubObj mode is enabled, highlights the sub-object (vertices, edges, polys, etc.) that will be selected. When Multi mode is enabled, any type of sub-object can be selected, and 3ds Max will automatically change sub-object modes to reflect the selection.

Edit Poly Selection rollout

Soft Selection

Soft selection allows the current selection to affect a wider area of the model by using a falloff. This allows the selection to be moved, but the rest of the model to deform smoothly as the selection is moved.

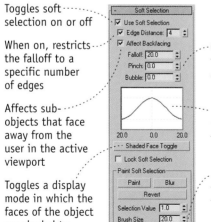

Toggles soft selection on or off

When on, restricts the falloff to a specific number of edges

Affects sub-objects that face away from the user in the active viewport

Toggles a display mode in which the faces of the object are shaded to represent the soft selection

Controls the falloff distance and rate

Provides a graphic representation of the falloff

Provides options for tools to paint the soft selection

Without soft selection, only the selected sub-objects are moved.

Soft selection allows the geometry surrounding the selection to deform smoothly when the selection is moved.

Editing Vertices

When vertices are the active sub-object, the Edit
Vertices rollout appears. These tools are specific
to vertices. To delete vertices, simply press the Delete
key. This can remove polygons from the object. If you
want to remove a vertex without affecting the model,
use the Remove button.

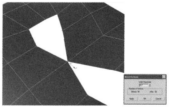

Remove Deletes selected vertices and combines the polygons
that use them.

Break Creates a new vertex for each polygon attached to
selected vertices, and disconnects the affected edges.

Extrude Extrudes the vertex.

Chamfer Chamfers the selected vertex.

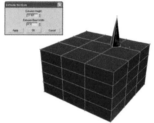

Weld Welds two vertices as one. Vertices must be within a
specified distance.

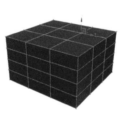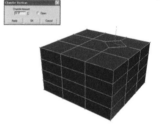

Target Weld Allows you to select a vertex and drag it over
another to weld the two together.

Connect Connects two vertices with an edge.

Editing Edges

When edges are the active sub-object, the Edit Edges rollout appears. These tools are specific to edges. To delete edges, simply press the Delete key. This can also remove polygons from the object, so if you want to remove a vertex without affecting the model, use the Remove button.

Remove Deletes selected edges and the polygons that use them.

Split Splits an edge or edges to create an open seam.

 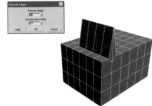 

Extrude Extrudes the edge.

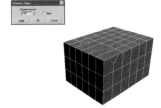

Chamfer Chamfers the selected edge.

 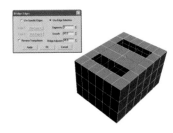 

Bridge Bridges the selected edges with new geometry.

Weld Welds two edges as one. Edges must be within a specified distance.

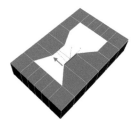 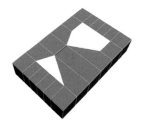

Target Weld Allows you to select an edge and drag it over another to weld the two together.

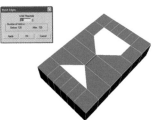 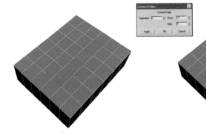

Connect Connects edges together with additional edges.

Editing Polygons

When polygons are the active sub-object, the Edit Polygons rollout appears. These tools are specific to polygons. To delete polygons, simply press the Delete key.

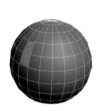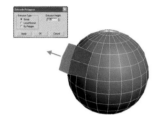

Extrude Extrudes a polygon along an axis

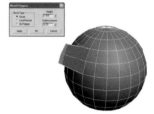

Bevel Extrudes, but also adds a bevel to control the size of the outline

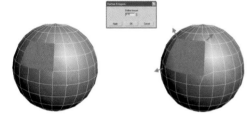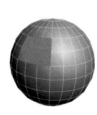

Outline Expands the selected faces while maintaining surface shape

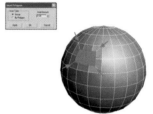

Inset Insets the selection

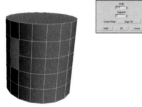

Hinge From Edge Extrudes a poly along a hinged edge

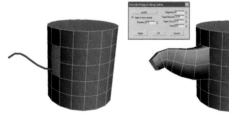

Extrude Along Spline Extrudes by using a user-selected spline

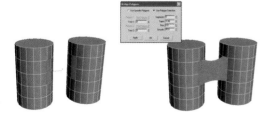

Bridge Connects selected polygons

Edit Geometry

The Edit Geometry rollout provides controls for modifying the geometry of the polygonal object, at either at the object or sub-object levels. Geometry can be created, and parts of the object can be hidden. The rollout also allows for objects to be attached or detached.

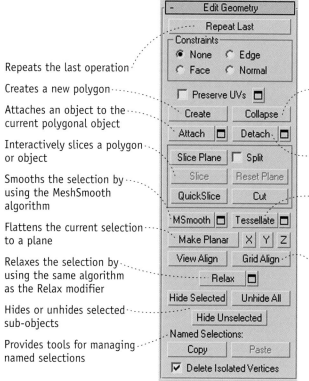

Repeats the last operation

Creates a new polygon

Attaches an object to the current polygonal object

Interactively slices a polygon or object

Smooths the selection by using the MeshSmooth algorithm

Flattens the current selection to a plane

Relaxes the selection by using the same algorithm as the Relax modifier

Hides or unhides selected sub-objects

Provides tools for managing named selections

Collapses selected sub-objects by welding their vertices at the selection center

Detaches selected sub-objects to a new polygonal object

Tessellates the selected sub-objects by using the same algorithm as the Tessellate modifier

Aligns all vertices in the object to the plane of the active viewport

Polygon: Material IDs

The Polygon: Material IDs rollout has controls for applying material IDs to the object and smoothing the object on a per-polygon basis. Material IDs allow multiple materials to be applied to a single object. Materials in a Multi/Sub-Object material will be applied to the polygons containing the corresponding ID. Smoothing groups control how the renderer calculates smoothing between the polygons, resulting in a smooth or faceted look.

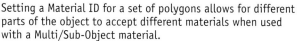

Setting a Material ID for a set of polygons allows for different parts of the object to accept different materials when used with a Multi/Sub-Object material.

The object on the left is smoothed by using smoothing groups; the one on the right has no smoothing. Smoothing can be applied on a per-polygon basis to smooth different parts of the object.

Paint Deformation

One additional way to reshape an object is by using the tools located in the
Paint Deformation rollout.

Sculpts the object
by pushing and/or
pulling detail

Reverts the action
of the brush to the
original state

Controls the
direction that
detail is pushed
or pulled

Brings up a Brush
Options dialog box
for fine-tuning the
brush behavior

Commits the changes
or cancels

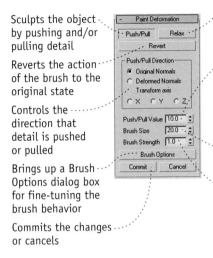

Relaxes detail
in the object by
using the brush

Determines how
strongly the
object is pulled
or pushed by
the brush

Indicates the size
of the brush

Determines a
multiplier that
affects the
push/pull and
relax behavior

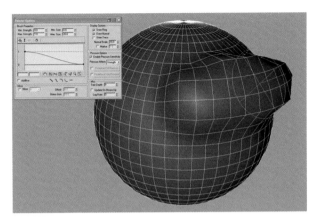

The Paint Deformation brush tools allow you to "sculpt" an
object interactively.

Modifying
Sub-Objects

Standard 3ds Max modifiers can be applied to
sub-objects so that they affect only part of an object.
An FFD, for example, can be applied to the nose of
a character to assist in reshaping it.

To apply a modifier to a sub-object selection,
the sub-object must be active when the modifier is
applied. The sub-object can be selected by using an
Edit Poly, Edit Mesh, or Edit Patch modifier. After the
modifier is applied, only the selection will be affected.
If needed, you can change the selection or add a
falloff by using soft selection to fine-tune the process.

If selection is all that's needed, a Select Poly,
Select Mesh, or Select Patch modifier will perform the
same task with less overhead.

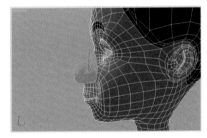

Using a Select Poly modifier, the polygons representing the
nose are selected.

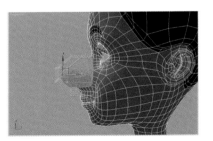

The FFD modifier is then added to the stack and affects only
those polygons in the selection.

Using Subdivision Surfaces

Subdivision surfaces combine the ease of polygonal modeling with the smoothness of a patch surface, giving you the best of both worlds. Subdivision surfaces are used extensively in character animation because they can define almost any complex smooth surface while keeping the underlying geometry light enough to be deformed quickly.

3ds Max has several ways to create a subdivision surface. The MeshSmooth and TurboSmooth modifiers can be applied to any editable poly or editable mesh object. Editable poly objects also have a subdivision surface built into the base object.

Subdivision surfaces allow the low-resolution character (left) to be smoothed (right).

MeshSmooth

The MeshSmooth modifier is the most common way of subdividing a mesh. The modifier has several algorithms that it can use to smooth out the mesh. Classic smooths the mesh to three- and four-sided faces, while Quad Output outputs only four-sided faces. The most robust and commonly used method is NURMS (non-uniform rational MeshSmooth), which allows for much more sophisticated control, such as weighting each control vertex. MeshSmooth also has the ability to apply smoothing in levels, so that part of an object can be smoothed differently than the rest.

Iterations control how much the mesh is subdivided. You can select different values for the iterations shown in the viewports and for the iterations that are actually rendered. Because the number of polygons in the object quadruples with each iteration, be careful about using high numbers for iterations.

The MeshSmooth modifier controls

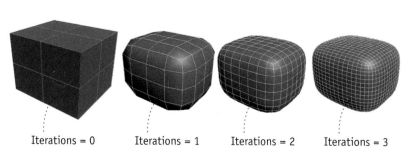

Iterations = 0   Iterations = 1   Iterations = 2   Iterations = 3

MeshSmooth allows you to see the underlying polygonal object as a "cage" superimposed on the smoothed object. The vertices and edges of this cage can be selected as sub-objects for the purposes of weighting, which can create creases or sharp edges.

Control edges　　Control vertices

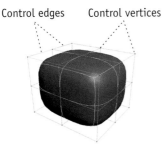

The control cage allows you to visualize how mesh is being smoothed as well as control parameters such as weighting and creasing.

Selecting a control vertex and increasing its weight draws the mesh toward it.

Selecting a control edge and adding a crease creates a corner.

By combining both methods, you can create sharp edges on an otherwise smooth mesh.

TurboSmooth

TurboSmooth is a simpler way to subdivide surfaces and will do much of the work of MeshSmooth without the overhead. It is much faster and more memory-efficient than MeshSmooth. It simply subdivides the mesh and allows you to set the iterations seen in the viewport and at rendering time. TurboSmooth also has an option for Explicit Normals, unavailable in MeshSmooth.

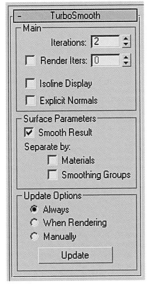

The TurboSmooth modifier is simpler and more efficient than MeshSmooth.

TurboSmooth does not create a control cage or allow for weighting of the mesh.

Smoothing Editable Polys

An editable poly object also has the ability to subdivide a surface. This option is available only in the editable poly object, but not in the Edit Poly modifier, so in order for this to be used, the stack must be collapsed to Editable Poly. The smoothing algorithm is based on MeshSmooth, and the controls are a subset of the modifier.

Because the smoothing using Editable Poly happens at the bottom of the stack, it works well for only certain types of objects, such as those that do not need additional modifiers in the stack. For applications such as character animation, the character is typically smoothed after skin and other deformation modifiers are added to the stack, so smoothing in the base object would not be applicable.

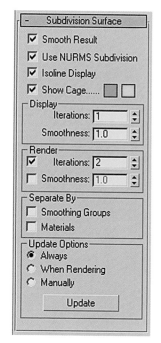

Editable poly objects have a Subdivision Surface rollout that can smooth the base object.

Creating Compound Objects

Compound objects combine two or more separate objects into a single object. Compound objects can be found under the Create menu or in the Create panel under the Geometry tab.

Compound objects work almost like modifiers, but without the stack. An object is selected, and then the compound object is applied to it, changing the object type. Additional objects are used to modify the compound object. After a compound object is created, it can be left in the compound state or it can be edited by using modifiers or by collapsing it to an editable object.

Booleans

A **Boolean object** is created by applying a Boolean operation on two objects. Booleans can be used to cut away, add, or intersect objects.

There are two ways to create Boolean objects: Boolean and ProBoolean. Boolean works on a pair of objects, while ProBoolean allows for multiple objects to be combined. Booleans are typically used for objects that are rigid. Booleans can create irregular edges where objects intersect, and these can become visible if the geometry is deformed.

Pro Boolean works in much the same way as Boolean, except you can select multiple objects to affect the original object. Pro Boolean can also automatically subdivide the Boolean result into quadrilateral faces, which lends itself well to smoothing edges with MeshSmooth and TurboSmooth.

The Boolean object allows for one object to modify another. The first object is selected and the Boolean object is applied. This places the object as operand A. The second object is selected as operand B. The type of operation can then be selected by using the parameters in the rollout.

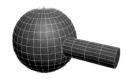

A sphere is selected as operand A, and a cylinder as operand B.

Union combines the two objects as one.

Intersection displays only those places where the two objects overlap.

Subtraction removes one object from the other. In this case, operand B is subtracted from operand A.

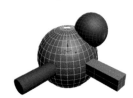

Cut creates a cut line of edges on the object.

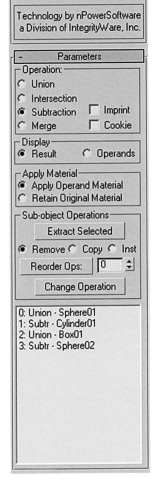

ProBooleans allows multiple objects to be combined. Once picked, the objects show up in the list at the bottom of the rollout.

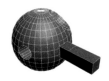

ProBooleans combines these objects by using different operations for each.

Scatter

The Scatter tool distributes a source object over a distribution object. This is useful for creating environments and scattering objects such as rocks and foliage across the ground surface. It can also be used for creating effects such as fur.

To scatter an object across a surface, select the source object and then select the scatter compound object. The distribution object is then selected within the Pick Distribution Object rollout. Scatter has a wide array of parameters to control the number of objects scattered and the way those objects are distributed.

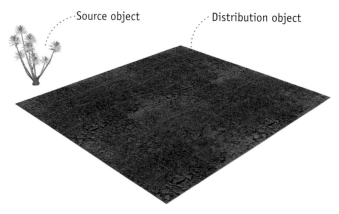

When using Scatter, the source object is scattered on the distribution object.

Scatter can control the number of objects, as well as their size and distribution.

Polygonal Modeling an Alien Character

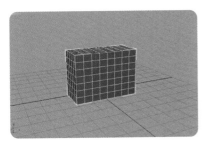

1 Start with a box and set the level of divisions at 8 × 7 × 5.

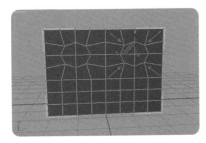

2 Add an Edit Poly modifier. Select these vertices and scale them to create the eye outlines.

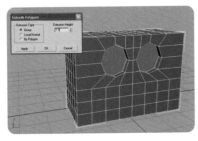

3 Select these polys and extrude them inward.

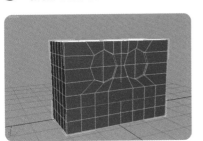

4 Select these edges to start creating the mouth.

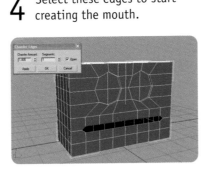

5 Chamfer the edges and select the Open check box to create a hole.

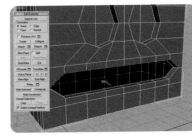

6 Select the border around the hole, hold down the Shift key, and drag the edge inward to create more detail for the mouth.

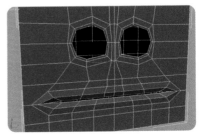

7 Continue this process to add detail to the mouth.

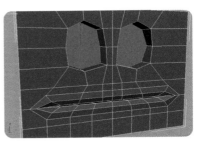

8 Select the polys inside the eye sockets and delete them.

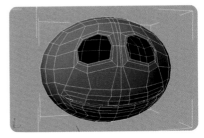

9 Using the same technique as for the mouth, reshape the eyes.

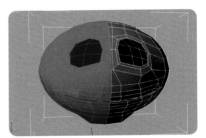

10 Add a Spherify modifier to round out the head.

11 Add another Edit Poly modifier. Select the polys on the right side of the head and delete them.

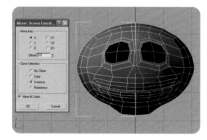

12 Select the head and use the Mirror command (Tools → Mirror) to instance a copy of the opposite side of the head.

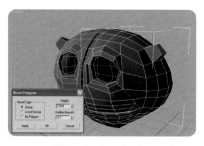

13 With the head mirrored, changes to one side affect the other. This allows you to tweak the shape of the head and keep the shape symmetrical. Select polys on the top of the head and use the Bevel tool to create antennae.

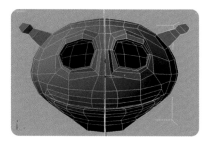

14 After the head is shaped to your satisfaction, recombine the two sides by using Attach. Select the polys on the reattached side and flip them.

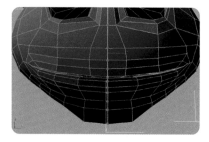

15 Select the vertices along the edges and use Weld to combine them. The head is pretty much done; now on to the body.

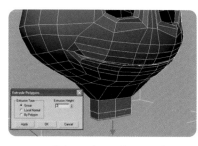

16 Select the polys on the underside of the head and extrude them to create a neck.

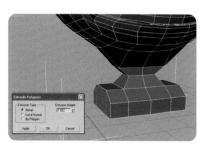

17 Select the polys on the outer edges of the neck and extrude them to create a shoulder.

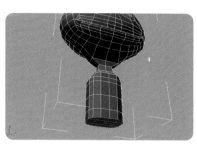

18 Select the polys on the underside of the neck and shoulders and extrude them to create a torso.

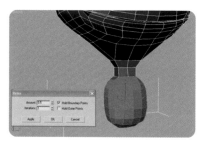

19 Select the polys that make up the torso and use Edit Poly's Relax tool to round it off.

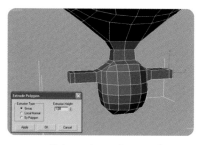

20 Select the polys on the edges of the shoulders and extrude them to create arms.

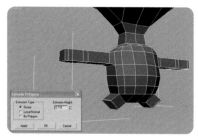

21 Select the polys on the underside of the torso and extrude them to create legs.

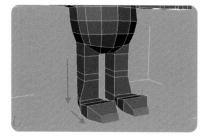

22 Reshape the detail on the extrusion and continue extruding to create legs and feet.

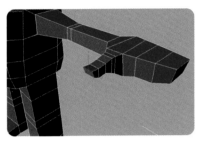

23 Select the polys on the ends of the arms and extrude them to create hands.

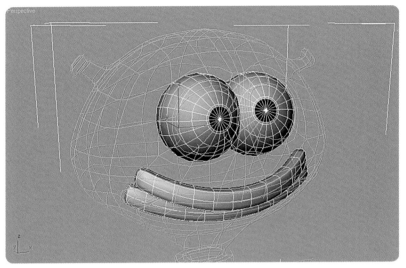

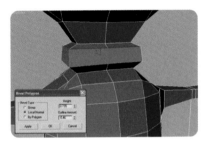

24 Select the polys on the neck. Open the Bevel tool and set it to Local Normal. Bevel these polys to create a collar.

26 Eyes are created by using simple spheres, and the teeth are created by using boxes with a Bend and MeshSmooth modifier added.

25 Add a MeshSmooth modifier to complete the body.

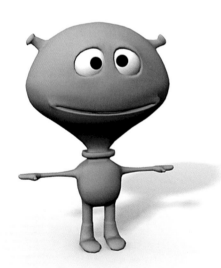

27 The character is done.

Spline Modeling a Spaceship

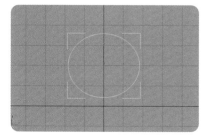

1 Start by creating a spline circle. Reshape this into a slight oval.

2 Hold down the Shift key and drag the circle to copy several times. Reshape these outlines to create the outline of the body.

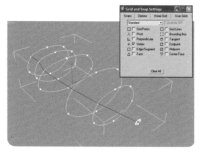

3 Open the Grid And Snap Settings window (Customize → Grid and Snap Settings) and enable Vertex snapping. Use the Line tool to draw a spline snapped to the edges of the circles.

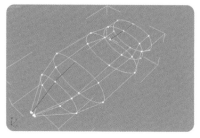

4 Continue doing this for the other outlines. The outline along the top needs to have a break around the cockpit area. Select the original circle, add an Edit Spline modifier, and attach all of the other splines to create a spline cage.

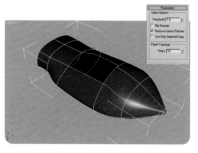

5 Add the Surface modifier to the cage. This will create patch surfaces along the splines. The body can be reshaped by adjusting the underlying splines or by adding an Edit Patch modifier.

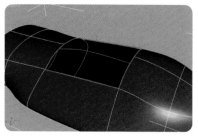

6 To create the rest of the cockpit, add an Edit Patch modifier to the stack and select the splines along the edge of the cockpit.

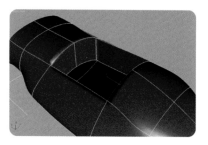

7 Hold down the Shift key and drag these edges down to extrude the detail.

8 Go into the stack and find the topmost Edit Spline modifier. Select the elliptical spline at the rear of the body. Hold down the Shift key and drag to duplicate this. Reselect this new shape and click Detach.

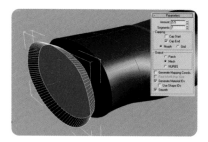

9 Add an Extrude modifier to this new curve to create the backplate. Turn off Cap Start and add a Taper modifier to the surface to taper it in slightly.

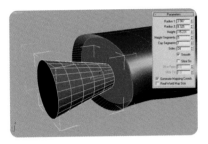

10 The rocket nozzle starts with a cone.

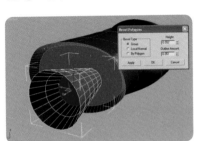

11 Add an Edit Poly modifier and extrude the end of the cone inward.

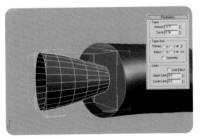

12 Add a Taper modifier to give it a rounder shape.

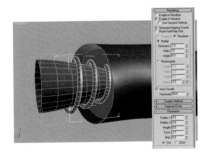

13 The cooling hoses are created with a Helix. Enable rendering in both the renderer and the viewport to give the curves volume.

14 Duplicate these two objects to create the second nozzle.

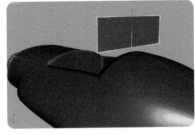

15 The windscreen is created by starting with a Quad Patch with a 1 × 2 subdivision.

16 Reshape the patch to match the outline of the body.

17 Select the splines on the outer edges of the windscreen to create the side detail.

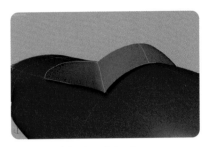

18 This detail is then reshaped.

19 The final spaceship is ready for texturing.

Creating Textures

Textures bring a model and a scene to life. Without texture, 3D models would appear rather dull and plastic. Textures add color, reflections, transparency, and roughness to a surface. In 3ds Max, you can create textures from bitmap files containing photographs, drawings, or paintings and also create textures by using tools to automatically generate textures.

3ds Max uses the Material Editor to create materials, which define the character of the surface. Each material can contain various textures, each defining one aspect of the surface, such as color, opacity, or roughness. Getting a texture to look the way you want can take a lot of revisions, so understanding how the Material Editor works is critical to mastering texturing within 3ds Max. In the production process, many times you create textures along with the lighting, because light has direct bearing on how a surface will look. Using tools such as 3ds Max's Activeshade can also help fine-tune textures much more quickly.

Working with Materials

Materials describe how an object reflects or transmits light, and define what the object will look like. A glass object will have a different material than a wooden one. Within a material, texture maps can be used to define the character of the surface, affecting parameters such as color, opacity, bump mapping, and reflectivity, among many others.

Material Editor

The heart of the texturing process is the Material Editor, which is the dialog box you use to create, alter, and apply the materials in your scene.

Material menu Displays options for getting and putting materials to libraries as well as previewing materials and activating or deactivating materials.

Materials Displays materials in these slots. Selecting a material slot allows you to edit its parameters.

Copy Material Makes a copy of the material so that the current slot can be edited without changing existing objects.

Get Material Gets a material from the library.

Apply Material Applies the material in the current slot to the selected objects.

Reset Material Resets the current material slot to the default parameters.

Pick Material Picks a material from an object and places it in the current slot.

Material Name Indicates the name of the current material. This can be changed by retyping the name.

Put To Library Saves the current material to the library.

Material ID Indicates the material ID. Each material can have a unique ID, which can be used to add rendering effects such as glows.

Material Parameters Indicates the parameters used in editing the material. These will change depending on the type of material selected.

Navigation menu Displays options for moving to and from parent nodes.

Options menu Displays options for changing the way materials are displayed and organized.

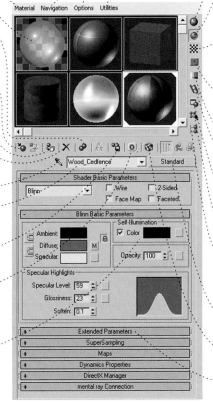

Utilities menu Displays options to select, condense, and reset materials.

Sample Type Allows you to preview your material on a sphere, cube, cylinder, or other object.

Backlight Shines a spotlight on the back of the material. Useful for transparent and glossy surfaces.

Background Adds a checkered background, which is useful in visualizing transparent surfaces.

Sample UV Tiling Changes the tiling of maps applied to the surface.

Color Check Checks for video-safe colors.

Make Preview Previews materials with animated textures.

Options Accesses a menu that changes display options.

Select By Material Selects objects that use the current material.

Material/Map Browser Brings up the Material/Map Browser window, where materials and maps can be browsed and selected.

Material Type Selects the type of material to be used.

Show Material Displays the object's material in the viewports

Rollouts Provides additional groups of parameters used to edit the material.

Options Menu

The Options menu allows you to customize the Material Editor. It lets you change the default lighting as well as create custom backgrounds and sample objects. It also has an option to increase the number of active material slots from 6 to a total of 24.

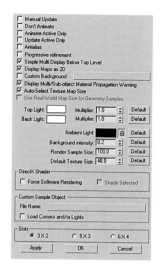

Material/Map Browser

Any time you change or create a material or map in the Material Editor, the Material/Map Browser appears. This window allows you to browse and select materials and maps.

3ds Max can store groups of maps and materials in libraries. Several libraries of common materials are supplied with the software, and these can make a good starting point for authoring your own materials. Many productions build their own custom materials libraries that contain materials specific to a project.

View Toggling these icons changes the view mode.

Browse Determines which materials and maps can be browsed.

Show Toggles the view of materials and maps. Those incompatible with the assigned renderer can also be shown.

Root Only Shows just the material, not the underlying maps that compose it.

File Options open, merge, and save material libraries.

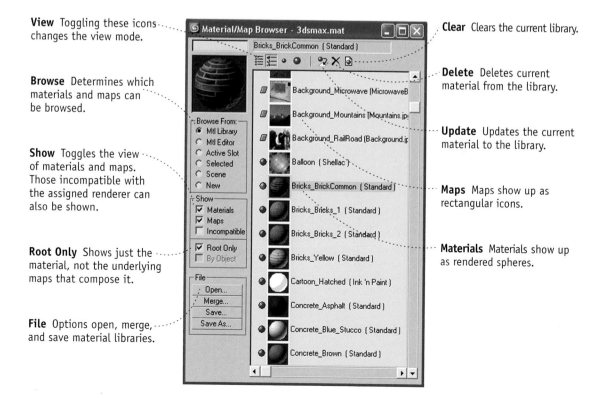

Clear Clears the current library.

Delete Deletes current material from the library.

Update Updates the current material to the library.

Maps Maps show up as rectangular icons.

Materials Materials show up as rendered spheres.

Creating and Editing Materials

Creating a material requires several steps. First, you need to decide the type of material to use. 3ds Max has many material types, which cover a wide range of surface types and options. After the basic material is selected, you can add textures and change parameters to fine-tune the material.

Each material has its own characteristics, depending on the type of surface and style of rendering. Materials can be added via plug-ins, so the number of different materials you may encounter can be quite robust. This section describes a few of the more common materials used within 3ds Max.

Standard Material

The standard material is the default material used in 3ds Max. It can simulate a wide variety of different surfaces by using different shading types. The shading types are selected by using a pull-down menu, and each type simulates a different type of surface and has its own set of parameters.

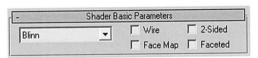

Shader The standard shader has a basic parameters rollout. This allows you to change the shading type as well as four other parameters. Wire renders the material in wireframe, 2-Sided renders the back side of a surface, Face Map maps a texture once per face of an object, and Faceted removes smooth shading calculations.

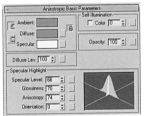 

Anisotropic Simulates surfaces that have directional highlights. Good for such materials as brushed metal, silk, and hair.

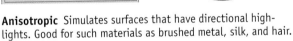 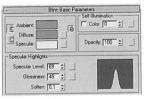

Blinn A versatile shading algorithm and probably the most popular among artists. Has fairly soft highlights by default.

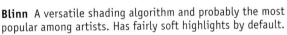

Metal A shader that resembles a metallic surface. Metal shading has a distinct curve for specular highlights. Metal surfaces also have glancing highlights. Metal materials calculate their own specular color based on the diffuse color and the color of the light, so you can't set it.

 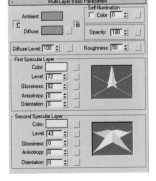

Multi-Layer A material that has two sets of anisotropic specular highlights. Good for creating surfaces that are highly polished or have depth, such as automobile paint.

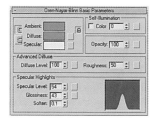

Oren-Nayar Blinn A softer version of the Blinn shader, this is good for nonreflective surfaces such as cloth.

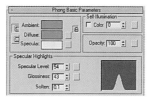

Phong One of the oldest shading algorithms, this creates a surface with distinct specular highlights. Supports reflections and is good for creating shiny artificial surfaces such as plastics and some glass.

Strauss A very simple shader mostly used to simulate plastic or metal surfaces.

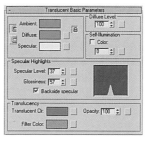

Translucent Translucent shading is similar to Blinn shading, but it also lets you specify translucency. A translucent object allows light to pass through, and also scatters light within the object. You can use translucency to simulate frosted and etched glass.

Raytrace Material

The Raytrace material uses 3ds Max's raytracer to render its surfaces. Raytracing works by tracing rays of light through the scene, which gives accurate reflections and refractions. This makes it ideal for transparent or reflective surfaces, such as glass or water.

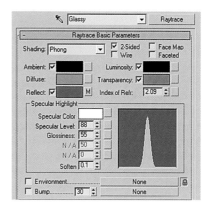

The Raytrace material allows for realistic reflections and refractions.

Matte/Shadow Material

The Matte/Shadow material is a special-purpose material used when compositing a 3D scene against existing images or footage. Objects textured with the Matte/Shadow material take on the look of the background image. These objects, however, can cast shadows and create reflections on the matte material, so that they can be used to integrate 3D objects.

The Matte/Shadow material can be used to place objects within images.

A model of a tree is placed against the image. The plane beneath it has a Matte/Shadow material applied.

When the scene is rendered, the Matte/Shadow material lets the background image show but adds the shadow of the tree.

The Matte/Shadow material has options to use atmospheres, as well as create shadows and reflections.

Multi/Sub-Object Material

This is not really a material, but a material that holds other materials. Each material has a list of sub-materials, which can be applied to different parts of an object. The parts of the polygon to be textured are configured in the Edit Poly or Edit Mesh modifier. In the polygon rollout, a polygon or group of polygons can be assigned an ID that corresponds to a sub-material slot. These polygons will be textured with the corresponding material.

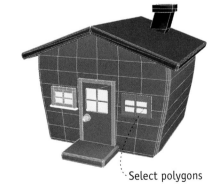

The Multi/Sub-Object material is used to apply multiple materials to a single object. Each sub-material has an ID number. The Window Frame material, for example, is ID number 2.

To apply this sub-material to the window frame of the house, apply an Edit Poly modifier and select the polygons that represent the window frame.

Within the Edit Poly modifier, you'll find a Polygon: Material IDs rollout. The material ID of these polygons can then be set to 2, so that the window frame will take the correct material.

Architectural Material

The Architectural materials are a robust set of materials that allow you to easily create surfaces used in architectural applications. These include glass, fabric, masonry, and metal, among others. Architectural materials are based on physical properties, so they provide high realism when rendered by using photometrics and radiosity, allowing architects and designers to create lighting studies with a high degree of accuracy.

　　Architectural materials, however, don't work well with the standard renderer or the light tracer.

Architectural materials offer a high degree of realism when used with radiosity- or photometric-based renderers.

Ink 'n Paint Material

The Ink 'n Paint material renders objects with a limited color palette along with an ink outline. This good for simulating the look of cel animation or doing illustrative work.

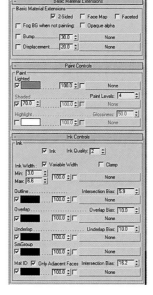

The Ink 'n Paint material has controls for the color of the paint, as well as controls for the color and quality of the ink strokes.

Mental Ray Material

The Mental Ray renderer will render most of 3ds Max's materials, but when it is assigned as the active renderer, a wider array of material types will become available. These include the Mental Ray material along with many other specialty materials.

Using Maps

Almost any parameter in any of the preceding shaders can be configured with a map. Maps can be created from bitmapped images, movie files, or procedurally. Maps can also contain other maps, creating nested trees of maps.

When working with maps, you'll need to navigate up and down through the maps and their component maps. You navigate by using the navigation icons in the Material Editor window.

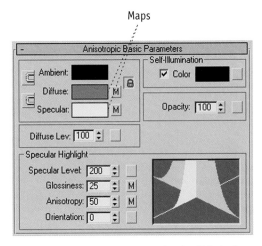

To place a map on a parameter, simply click the box to the right of the parameter and select the desired map type from the Material/Map window.

Maps can also be added and modified by using the Maps rollout in the Material Editor.

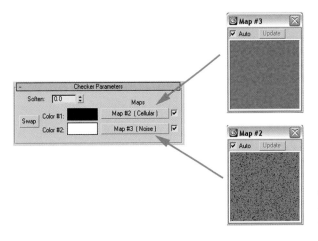

Maps can contain other maps. The colors in this simple checkerboard pattern can be replaced with maps for a more-complex look.

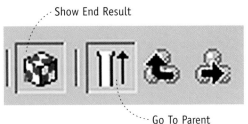

To navigate through the various maps, use the navigation buttons.

Mapping Color

One of the more common parameters to map is color. Most shaders use three parameters for color: Diffuse, Ambient, and Specular.

The **Specular** channel is the color of the object's highlights. Maps on the Specular channel can give the surface a sense of "roughness."

The **Diffuse** channel is the "main" color of the object. This is where bitmaps or procedural textures are added to give the object its character.

The **Ambient** channel is the color of an object in those places where it is in shadow. Typically, this parameter is locked to the Diffuse channel.

Mapping Opacity

Opacity maps change the transparency of an object. They can be used to create glass- or water-like effects. Varying the transparency by using gradients or falloff maps can give the appearance of varying thicknesses.

This bitmap is used to create an Opacity map that, when mapped on a plane, creates a cobweb.

Mapping Self-Illumination

Self-Illumination maps create the illusion of incandescence by replacing any shadows on the surface with the diffuse color. This is good for simulating glowing surfaces and can also be used to remove shadowed areas on an object.

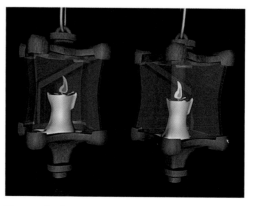

The candle flame on the right has self-illumination applied.

Mapping Bumps

Bump maps give a surface a sense of roughness and depth. Most surfaces are not perfectly smooth, and a little bit of bump mapping can go a long way toward making objects seem real. It is also easier and more efficient to add surface imperfections by using Bump or Displacement maps than to actually model every bump and pockmark on a surface.

Bump mapping only affects the way light interacts with the surface, but does not actually modify geometry; so the edges still appear smooth. Bump mapping is perfectly fine for creating general surface roughness or more-exaggerated bumps on surfaces such as a ground plane or a wall.

Bump mapping affects the character of a surface but does not modify the geometry. The edges of this sphere are not distorted.

Mapping Displacement

Displacement mapping changes the surface of the geometry, adding another level of realism. This process takes more processing and rendering power, so use displacements only where they are needed and use bumps for the rest. Because displacement mapping physically changes the geometry, the spinner to the left of the map is the height of the displacement. Displacement also distorts the actual geometry of the object, so higher-resolution geometry might be needed.

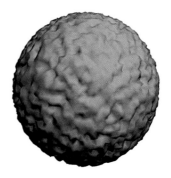

Displacement affects the geometry; notice how the edges are displaced.

Mapping Reflections

Any shiny object reflects light. Reflections are important in simulating reality. A mirror might reflect an image perfectly, whereas galvanized metal might reflect only broad swaths of color, but they both reflect at least a little bit of their environment.

The most accurate form of reflections comes from using the Raytrace map, but many artists simply use bitmapped environments. Although not as accurate, bitmapped environments can be much faster to render, and, in most cases, reflections do not need to be completely accurate to sell the illusion of reality. If there is no "real" environment, such as when an object is rendered by itself, bitmap environments are a necessity. They are particularly useful when creating animation that integrates with film or video. Artists who work on special effects often take photographs of the film sets in order to generate bitmap reflections.

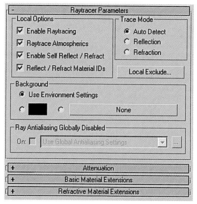

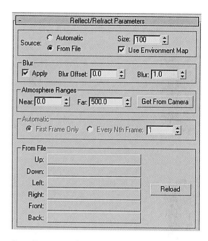

This object appears to be made of chrome because it reflects its environment. These reflections were created by using a Raytrace map, so actual objects in the environment are reflected.

Reflections generated by using the Raytrace map do not need mapping, because the reflection is generated directly from the objects in the scene. The reflectivity attribute of the material determines the amount of light the surface reflects.

Another mapping type is the Reflect/Refract map, which is faster and simpler than the Raytrace map. This map works by using six renderings in the form of a cube that surrounds the objects. These renders are then applied as reflections.

Mapping Refractions

Refractions are used for semitransparent objects to simulate how light bends, or refracts, through a surface. There are two main ways to calculate refractions in the default 3ds Max renderer: with the Raytrace map and the Reflect/Refract map.

The main parameter to use is the index of refraction (IOR) value. This will change, depending on the type of surface. In the Raytrace material, this is adjusted in the map, while in the Raytrace and Reflect/Refract maps, it is adjusted in the Extended Parameters rollout.

Refractions simulate how light bends as it passes through a surface, much like a lens.

Types of Maps

3ds Max has a wide variety of maps. These fall into two main categories: 2D and 3D maps. 2D maps contain bitmaps and other types of maps that create images defined by two dimensions, and are mapped by using U and V coordinates. 3D maps also have depth and are calculated volumetrically. They're mapped by using UVW coordinates.

Maps can also fall into two other categories, bitmaps and procedural:

Bitmap textures are derived from image or movie files. These can have a wide variety of formats. Because bitmaps are external files, you need to manage these separately.

Procedural textures create images by using custom algorithms. These can create all sorts of natural looks and phenomena. You can map them to any object by using UV coordinates, and you can also tile them. Procedural textures can be useful because they can create natural-looking effects quickly and with little overhead. You can also animate procedural textures by keyframing their attributes.

3ds Max has a wealth of procedural textures, and you can add to the list by using third-party plug-ins. Here are a few of the more common procedural textures:

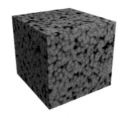

Cellular A map that simulates natural phenomenon such as mosaic tiles, bumpy skin, pebbled surfaces, and more.

Checker A map that creates a two-color checkerboard pattern.

Gradient A map that creates a linear or circular three-color gradient.

Gradient Ramp A map that creates a user-definable gradient with as many colors as desired.

Noise A map that creates Gaussian or fractal noise.

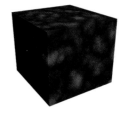

Smoke A map that simulates smoke. It is usually used to create opacity maps for clouds and other smoky effects.

Splat A map that simulates splattered paint.

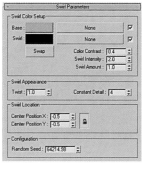

Swirl A map that creates a swirl effect.

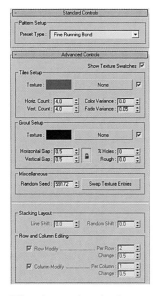

Tiles A map that simulates a wide variety of tiling and brick patterns.

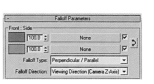

Falloff A map that changes color depending on the angle of view. This is really good for simulating transparencies as well as surfaces such as silk.

Applying Materials

After a material is created, it can be applied to an object. Applying a material is as simple as right-clicking and dragging it from the Material Editor window to the object. The Assign Material icon or menu option can also be used to assign a material to the selected object or objects.

Mapping

In order for a material to appear on a surface, it needs to be mapped. Most objects in 3ds Max have default mapping coordinates assigned, but many times these will not suffice. 3ds Max has several tools to modify an object's mapping coordinates.

Coordinates Rollout

The first way to modify how a texture will map is within the texture itself. Every map will have a Coordinates rollout, which adjusts how the map is applied to the surface. It allows you to tile a map, move and rotate a map relative to the surface, and mirror a map, among other tasks.

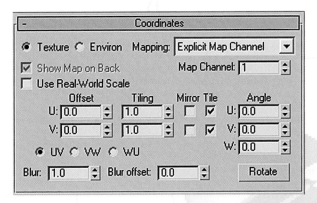

Texture tiling can be changed in the material's Coordinates rollout.

UVW Map

The next most common mapping method is by adding the UVW Map modifier to the stack. This modifier can map a texture to an object in several different ways.

Just as with any modifier, the UVW Map modifier can be used to affect sub-objects. This allows you to map different parts of an object with different mapping coordinates.

To do this, simply add an Edit Poly or Select Poly modifier in the stack, and select the polys you want to map. Leave the sub-object open and add the UVW Map modifier to map just the selected sub-objects.

The UVW Map modifier. Mapping can be adjusted by using the parameters in the modifier. The gizmo can also be selected and manipulated by moving, rotating, and scaling.

Planar Maps the image to a projection plane

Cylindrical Maps the image to a cylinder

Spherical Maps the image to a sphere

Shrink Wrap Maps the image to a sphere, but without pinching the poles

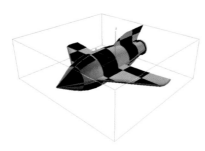

Box Maps the image to the six faces of a box

Face Maps the image as one image per face

Unwrap UVW

One of the big benefits of polygonal modeling is that polygonal objects can have branches and multiple surfaces. This, however, makes it difficult to texture them with simple projections or 2D image placement.

The Unwrap UVW modifier is the best way to edit texture mapping on a complex polygonal object. It allows you to lay a wireframe representation of the object against a texture map and place textures exactly by adjusting the positions of the object's UV coordinates.

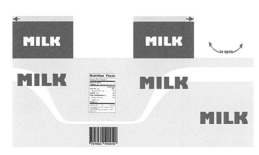

The texture map contains images for all parts of the object. This map is placed inside a material and applied to the object.

The Unwrap UVW modifier is added to the object.

The final result is perfectly mapped.

Tools menu Tools on this menu let you flip and mirror texture coordinates, weld vertices, combine and separate sets of texture coordinates, and sketch outlines for multiple selected vertices.

Mapping menu Lets you apply automatic, procedural mapping methods to a model. Each method provides settings so you can adjust the mapping to the geometry you're using.

Map Selection Selects a map to display in the viewport.

File menu Options to load, save, and reset UVW coordinates.

Edit menu Commands that provide access to the different transform functions, and copy-and-paste selections.

Select menu Commands that let you copy a viewport selection to the editor, and transfer selections among the three different sub-object modes.

Move/Rotate/ Scale Tools to let you move, rotate, and scale selected parts of the object.

Editing viewport This is where the mapping of the object is matched to the bitmap. This can be navigated like a standard ortho-graphic viewport.

View menu Options to pan and zoom within the viewport.

Display menu Options to hide, freeze, and show various parts of the viewport.

Options menu Options for setting defaults.

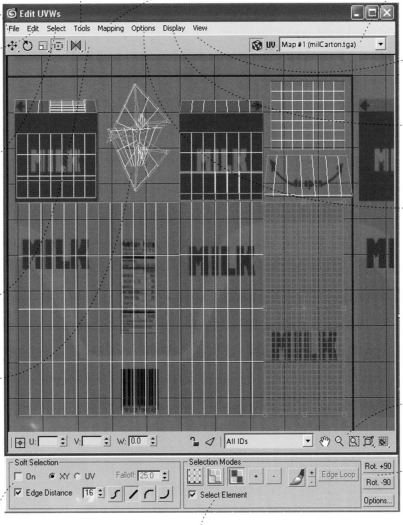

Navigation tools Tools to navigate the Editing viewport.

Rotate 90 These will rotate the current selection by 90 degrees.

Soft Selection Tools to soft-select the geometry of the object.

Selection modes Options to select by vertex, edge, or polygon. You can also select by element and paint selections.

The UVW Editor allows you to select parts of the object and position them so they match up with the bitmap.

Polygonal Modeling an Alien Character

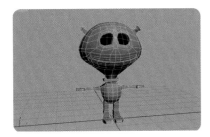

1 Open the file Alien_Start.max. This has the character modeled in Chapter 2.

2 Create a Multi/Sub-Object material. Set the number of slots to 4 and apply this material to the character.

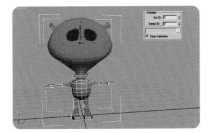

3 Select the polys that compose the character's head. Use the Set ID spinner to set the Material ID to 1.

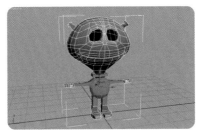

4 Select the polys that make up the body, and set the ID on them to 2. Do the same for the boots (ID = 3) and the gloves (ID = 4).

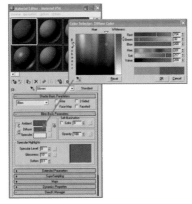

5 Now create the individual materials for the body parts. Start with the gloves. Select the material in the last slot and give it the name **Gloves**. Add a color to the Diffuse channel.

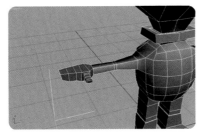

6 Notice how the change in color of the material affects only the polys that have the corresponding material ID.

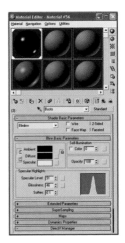

7 Now create the material for the Boots in slot 3. For this material, add some shininess by increasing the Specular Level and Glossiness.

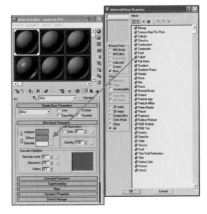

8 Now for the skin texture. Use the material in slot 1. Add a Falloff map to the Diffuse slot.

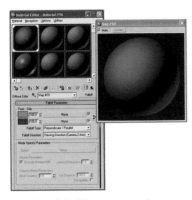

9 The falloff changes color depending on the angle of view, giving a richer look. Add a light turquoise and a dark blue color to the respective channels.

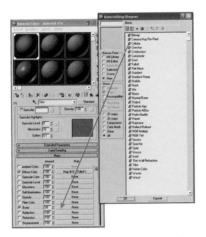

10 The skin needs to be a bit bumpy. Add a Cellular map to the Bump channel.

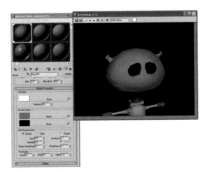

11 To tweak this map, it's best to view it on the character. Open an ActiveShade window so you can see how the material renders as you edit the

parameters. Adjust the size of the Cellular map and the amount of bump to your liking.

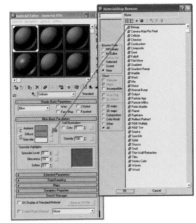

12 Now let's create the material for the character's uniform. Select the material on slot 2 and add a Bitmap modifier to the Diffuse channel.

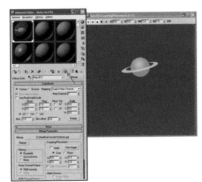

13 Select the file Uniform.jpg as the bitmap. To display the bitmap on the character, click the Show Map in Viewport icon.

14 The map will probably not match the character. We need to adjust this.

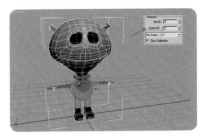

15 Select the polys that compose Material ID 2. This can be done manually or by using the Select ID button.

16 With the polys selected, add a UVW Map modifier to the stack. Because the polys are selected, the modifier will affect only that part of the model. Set the mapping type to Planar and highlight Gizmo.

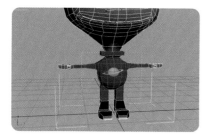

17 Adjust the Gizmo in the viewport to place the map, and then use the Length and Width parameters to scale it.

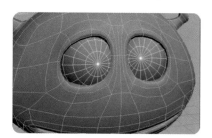

18 Now create textures for the eyes. Select Unhide All to reveal the eyes, which are simple spheres.

19 Create a Multi/Sub-Object material with two slots. The first slot is black; the second is white. Apply this material to the eyes.

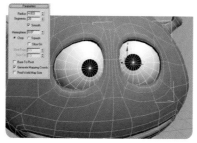

20 Select each eye and adjust the Hemisphere spinner to create the pupils.

21 The final character.

4

Lighting

ny photographer will tell you how important lighting is when taking a photograph. In the basic sense, photography is nothing more than capturing and recording light. Artists working in 3ds Max also use light, but because 3ds Max uses a digital representation of light, you can do things with light that are impossible in nature. In 3ds Max, you can switch a light's shadows on or off, vary the intensity of light according to distance, and create lights that actually remove light from a scene. 3ds Max also provides methods to create highly realistic and natural lighting, simulating the way real light propagates through an environment. These tools give you the freedom to create the real world or your own world.

Lighting Makes the Image

Proper lighting is one of the foundations of a great image. The color, character, and amount of light in a scene sets the mood and gives the audience a lot of information about where and when the action is happening. Light tells people the difference between day and night or lets them know whether something is scary, moody, or friendly. Light also helps define the form and shape of an object. Good lighting makes a good model look great, while poor lighting can make the best models look average.

A scene with one light. The lighting in this scene is flat and does not do much to sell the image to the audience.

By adding a few lights and some color, we can set a mood.

Changing the lighting can quickly change the mood and tone of the scene.

Creating Lights

The various types of lighting can be accessed by choosing Create → Lights or by selecting the light icon in the Create panel. 3ds Max has two main categories of lights: standard and photometric. The types of lights you select will depend on the application and type of renderer you select. Standard lights are used with 3ds Max's scanline renderer and with the

Mental Ray renderer. They are the choice for animation and most other applications. Photometric lights are used with the scanline renderer's radiosity feature to create accurate lighting for architectural applications.

Standard lights are used for most applications and can create a wide range of lighting, from highly realistic to highly stylized.

Architectural applications need highly accurate lighting that simulates the real world. Photometric lighting is perfect for creating these types of images.

Light Parameters

Standard lights have the same parameter rollouts used to create and define the character of the light.

Options to set the type of light, turn it on/off, and create a target for aiming the light.

Options to set the type of shadow as well as turn shadows on or off.

A value that multiplies the intensity of the light. This value can be negative to remove light from the scene.

Values used to attenuate the light close to the source.

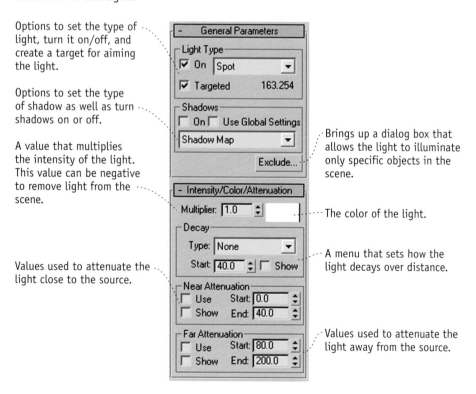

Brings up a dialog box that allows the light to illuminate only specific objects in the scene.

The color of the light.

A menu that sets how the light decays over distance.

Values used to attenuate the light away from the source.

Types of Lights

Different parts of the scene may need different types of lights. Some parts of the scene may need a general wash of light, while others may need a spotlight directed at a specific object. 3ds Max provides a wide collection of lighting types to fit all needs.

Spotlights originate from a single point and spread outward in a conical shape. 3ds Max has two types of spotlights: Target Spot and Free Spot. The only difference is that a Target Spot has the target attribute turned on, which creates a target that the user can manipulate to control the direction of the spot. Spotlights can illuminate both diffuse and specular areas of a scene. They also can cast shadows and decay over distance. Hotspot/Beam adjusts the size of the entire light; Falloff/Field controls the softness of the edge of the light cone. Spotlights can be either circular or rectangular.

Omni lights can be thought of as bare lightbulbs in the room. Like a lightbulb, an omni light sends its rays in every direction. Similar to spotlights, omni lights affect the specularity of an object and can cast shadows. The best use for an omni light is as an overall scene light.

Directional lights are similar to spotlights in that they have a specific direction, but a directional light does not emanate from a single point. Instead, the rays are parallel and simulate distant lights such as the sun. This makes them ideal for outdoor scenes. This light also comes in two varieties, Target Direct and Free Direct, the only difference being the target.

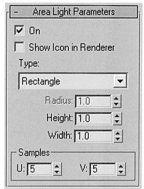

Area lights cast their light from an area, rather than from a point. These are only available only to the Mental Ray renderer. This makes them a good choice for simulating diffuse lighting, bounce lights, or fluorescent tubes. Although area lights can provide realistic effects, calculating complex shadows can eat up a lot of render time.

Skylights are a special type of light that simulates natural diffuse lighting. This light is great for adding realism to a scene, but it does take longer to render. When using a skylight, the Light-Tracer must be turned on in the Render Scene dialog box.

Mental Ray Lights

Directional, point, and spotlights in 3ds Max can be used with the Mental Ray for 3ds Max renderer, and most 3ds Max lighting parameters translate with no effort. Each light has rollouts for the mental ray options, which control indirect illumination and light shaders. Indirect illumination in mental ray simulates the way light naturally moves through a scene. Global illumination (GI) simulates how light bounces off surfaces in a scene and can create very soft and realistic renderings. Caustics simulates the way light transmits through an object or reflects off it. Light shaders are custom plug-ins for mental ray that affect the light's behavior for creating special effects.

Normally, mental ray takes the shadow map information from the 3ds Max light panel. This panel allows you to control the settings manually.

Sets the energy or intensity of the light for indirect illumination calculations.

Specifies how photon energy decays as it moves away from the light source.

Sets the number of caustic photons used when calculating how light transmits through an object or reflects off it.

Sets the number of photons used to calculate global illumination.

Parameters for calculating indirect illumination, which simulates real-world lighting.

Settings to multiply the default indirect illumination parameters set in the Render Scene dialog box.

These are custom plug-ins for mental ray that affect the light's behavior for creating special effects.

Adjusting Lights

Lights can be manipulated by using the Modify panel or directly in a viewport. Lights can be aimed and positioned by using the Move and Rotate tools, and if a light has a target, the target can be moved as well. The Select And Manipulate tool can be used to adjust the cone angle and rotation of a spotlight or direct light.

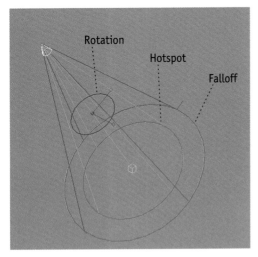

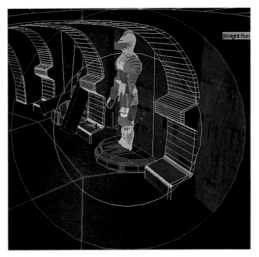

Adjusting light parameters by using the Select And Manipulate tool.

Another way to adjust spotlights and direct lights is to look through them, much like a camera. Use the Views option in a viewport's pull-down menu to select the light and see the scene from the light's view. You can use camera navigation tools to position the light.

Creating Shadows

Almost all objects cast shadows, and creating realistic shadows is one of the keys to truly simulating reality in 3ds Max. Shadows not only add realism, but contribute greatly to the mood of a scene; they help the eye determine the placement of objects in a scene, and they visually anchor objects to the ground.

Shadows add to the realism of the scene and help anchor objects to the ground.

Raytraced shadows (left) render shadows through transparent objects, but depth map shadows (right) won't.

Shadow Parameters

Parameters affecting all types of shadows can be adjusted with the Shadow Parameters rollout in the light's Modify panel. These parameters affect the color of the shadow as well as the density of the shadow. You can also have atmospheric effects cast shadows.

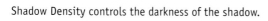

Shadow Density controls the darkness of the shadow.

Shadows can also be given color.

Depth Map Shadows

Depth map shadows are used extensively by artists because they render quickly. Though not quite as precise as raytraced shadows, they're great for most general shadowing applications. 3ds Max creates a depth map shadow by rendering one or more bitmaps showing the depths of the scene from the light's point of view. 3ds Max will then compare these bitmaps with the

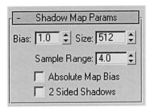

objects in the scene to determine which areas are in the shadow. To control this process, 3ds Max provides a Shadow Map Params rollout to adjust these parameters.

The two most important parameters to understand when working with depth map shadows are the Size and the Sample Range parameters. The Size parameter determines the size of the shadow map, which covers the width of the light cone. The Sample Range parameter controls the soft edge of the shadow. The larger the size of the shadow map, the more accurate the shadow. The larger the sample range, the more softening. Softening, however, is relative to the resolution, so larger size maps require more filtering to get the same softness.

Although large maps are more accurate, they take up more memory when rendering. The size of the map depends on the cone angle of the light. If the light covers an area the size of the image, the depth map should be approximately the size of the image. Sometimes

Size = 256, Sample Range = 1.

Size = 256, Sample Range = 4.

Size = 512, Sample Range = 1.

Size = 512, Sample Range = 4.

Size = 1024, Sample Range = 1.

Size = 1024, Sample Range = 1.

smaller maps are preferred, because they can produce softer shadows with less filtering.

There are other parameters you can set in this rollout. Two-sided shadows will render shadows for both sides of a surface. Bias is a parameter that offsets the shadow from the object by a small amount to ensure that the shadow is behind the object. If the parameter is too low, parts of the shadow will render in front of the object. If it is too high, the shadow will be offset from the object.

When Bias is set to a high value (right), the shadow is offset from the object.

Raytraced Shadows

Raytraced shadows work by tracing the actual beams of light through the scene. This is more computationally expensive than simple depth map shadows, but raytraced shadows prove to be more accurate. They can create shadows for transparent objects, and they are also easier to set up, because you do not have to calculate map sizes. 3ds Max has two types of raytraced shadows: regular and advanced. The Advanced Raytraced Shadows option has additional parameters for controlling the look of the shadow.

The Ray Traced Shadow Params rollout has options to control the bias of the shadow, which is very similar to the bias control on depth map shadows. You can also use this rollout to turn on two-sided shadows.

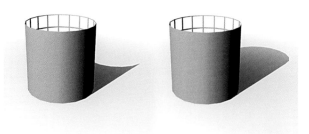

When the 2 Sided Shadows option is turned on (right), the rear-facing sides of the surface (wire) will also cast shadows.

Advanced Raytraced Shadows

Advanced raytraced shadows are an improvement on standard raytraced shadows. These shadows have additional parameters to control the softness of the shadow, along with controls to optimize transparency and shadow calculation.

Antialias Type Determines the antialiasing algorithm: Simple, 1-Pass, or 2-Pass. Simple is the fastest to render, but 2-Pass produces the highest-quality shadows and will take a spotlight's falloff into consideration.

The number of shadow rays cast from a surface.

The number of secondary rays cast from a surface.

Allows transparency of objects to affect the shadow. Turning this on will increase render times.

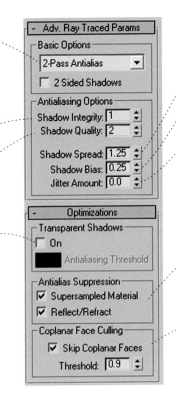

Determines the softness of the shadow.

Moves the shadow away from the object to prevent overlap.

Randomizes the rays to create a more-realistic soft shadow.

Suppresses antialiasing for supersampled materials and reflections. Turning these options off can increase render times.

Prevents coplanar faces from shadowing each other.

By default, raytraced shadows have fairly crisp edges.

Advanced Raytraced Shadows can soften the edges by using Shadow Spread. The image on the left has a value of 12, the one on the right a value of 48. If the value gets too high, the samples will start to show.

The Jitter option adds randomness to enhance the realism of the shadow. Typical values range from 0.25 to 1.0, but they can go higher if needed.

Creating Lighting Effects

Lighting Effects add realism to the way the light illuminates the scene. Adding decay and attenuation simulates the way a real-world light's energy falls off with distance. These parameters can also be used to play with reality and place or remove light from the scene.

Decay

By default, lights in 3ds Max illuminate all objects equally, no matter how far they are from the light. In the real world, however, the intensity of a light decays with distance. To create more-natural lighting that falls off over distance, you can select Decay in the light's Intensity/Color/Attenuation rollout. There are two types of decay:

Inverse falls off directly with distance.

Inverse Square falls off as the square of the distance. This is the same as real-world lighting.

When decay is added to a light, you almost always need to increase the intensity of the light to illuminate the scene. When using Inverse Square decay, you may have to increase the light intensity by several orders of magnitude to illuminate the scene. One way to offset this is to use the Start parameter, which specifies a discrete distance from the light where the decay starts.

By default, lights in 3ds Max illuminate all areas of the scene equally. The spotlight in this scene illuminates the last chess piece as much as the first.

When Decay is set to Inverse, the light falls off as it reaches the last piece.

When Decay is set to Inverse Square, the light falls off more quickly.

Attenuation

Another way to control the way light changes over distance is to use near and far attenuation. These are much more controllable than just simple decay and allow you to set ranges for the decay of the light when it gets close or far from the source. Attenuation is terrific for putting light into specific places in a scene.

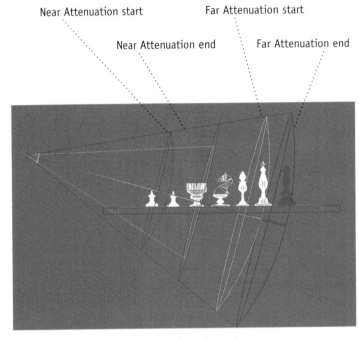

Near Attenuation start   Far Attenuation start

Near Attenuation end   Far Attenuation end

Near Attenuation
☑ Use   Start: 2.633
☑ Show   End: 152.57

Far Attenuation
☑ Use   Start: 267.4
☑ Show   End: 404.92

By selecting Show in the Attenuation rollout, attenuation can be shown in a viewport.

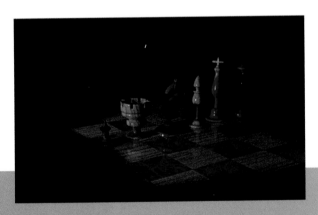

The result is a light that can vary according to distance. In this case, the light is attenuated both near to the source and far from it, so only the middle chess pieces are illuminated.

Advanced Lighting Effects

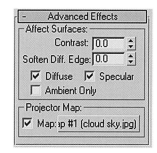

The Advanced Effects rollout contains additional parameters to control the character of a light. Lights can be configured to have more contrast or to soften, as well as to illuminate only ambient, diffuse, or specular parts of the scene. These effects can be handy when lighting a scene, because you can configure a light to add contrast, softness, or ambient lighting to anything it illuminates.

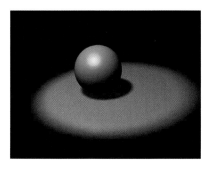

Basic lighting on a sphere contains diffuse and specular lighting.

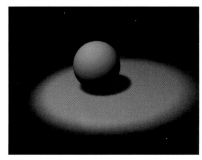

Diffuse-only lighting illuminates the shape of the object.

Specular-only lighting illuminates just the highlights.

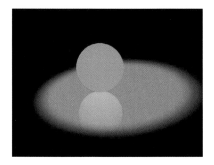

Ambient-only lighting adds ambient light to the scene.

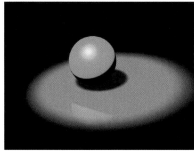

A light can also illuminate with more contrast...

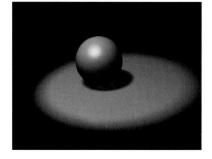

...or more softness.

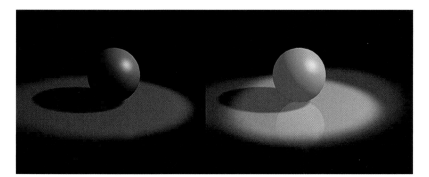

These effects are best used in conjunction with other lights. In this case, a standard spotlight is used (left) and an ambient-only spotlight is added (right) to brighten up the dark spots on the sphere.

Lights can also be used to project images on parts of the scene, much like a slide projector. This is accomplished by using a map in the Color channel. This can be anything from a bitmap to a procedural texture, such as a ramp.

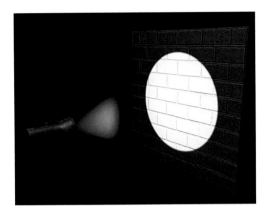 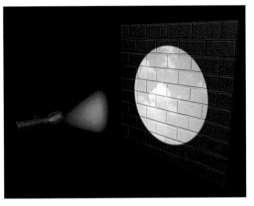

The spotlight in this scene is set to be used as a projector to cast an image. The bitmap of the sky is placed in the spotlight's Color channel, and the result casts the sky on the backdrop.

Atmospheres and Effects

3ds Max offers several ways to add special effects to lights. These effects can be loaded by using the Atmospheres & Effects rollout in the light's Modify panel. Each light can have multiple effects added, and third-party effects can also be loaded as plug-ins. 3ds Max comes with two ways to affect a light: volume lights and lens effects.

In the Atmospheres & Effects rollout, the Add and Delete buttons apply the effects. The Setup button allows you to modify the highlighted effect via the Environment And Effects window.

Volume Light

One way to make lights more visible is to use volume light, which simulates the effect of light through a dusty or smoky room. Volume light can be used on spotlights, direct lights, or omni lights. Fog in a spotlight takes up a cone shape, but omni light fog can have a specific radius and falloff, for creating fog in a specific volume.

Selected effect Effects placed on a light show up in this list. Select the light to configure the effect.

Allows you to choose which light to apply to the effect.

Indicates the color of the volume light's fog as well as the attenuation color, which changes over distance.

Turns on shadow casting within the fog.

Attenuates the effect as a percentage of the light's attenuation settings.

Adds noise to the volume effect to simulate smoky or cloudy effects.

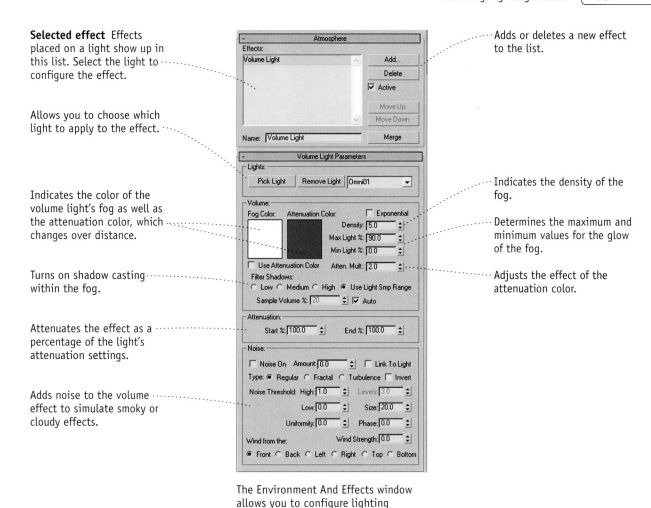

Adds or deletes a new effect to the list.

Indicates the density of the fog.

Determines the maximum and minimum values for the glow of the fog.

Adjusts the effect of the attenuation color.

The Environment And Effects window allows you to configure lighting effects, such as volume light.

A volume light creates a fog effect on the light.

When combined with shadows, fog can create some dramatic effects.

Lens Effects

Many times you need to make a light source visible. To do so, you use 3ds Max's Lens Effects, a suite of effects that allow you to add effects such as glow, halos, and lens flares to a light. Like Volume Lights, Lens Effects are added by using the Atmospheres & Effects rollout in the light's Modify panel. The Lens Effects main window has tools to globally control the size of the effect as well as to render tests.

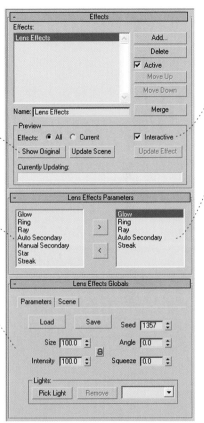

Interactively updates the effects as the parameters are tuned.

Active effects The effects that are actually applied to the light. Highlight an effect to edit.

Allows you to preview the effect.

Available effects A list of available effects for the light, Highlight an effect and click the right arrow button to add it to the list of available effects.

Parameters for setting the overall size and intensity of the effects. Individual effects are adjusted in their own rollouts.

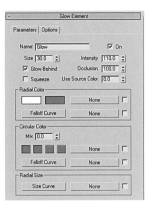

This scene has an omni light to which Lens Effects is applied.

When a glow is added, the light becomes visible.

Additional effects include rings, streaks, and rays.

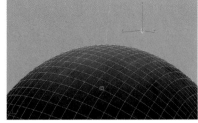

Each effect has its own rollout for customizing its behavior.

Setting Light Exclusion

Light exclusion gives you precise control over lighting on an object-by-object basis. Lists of objects can be excluded from a specific light or can be included. This gives you many ways to customize how lights affect the scene. The window is accessed by clicking the Exclude button on the light's General Parameters rollout.

A list of all the objects in the scene. To include or exclude an object, simply highlight it and click the right arrow button to add it to the list of excluded or included objects.

This toggles whether the objects in the list are included or excluded.

Determines whether the light excludes or includes illumination, shadows, or both.

A list of objects to be included or excluded from the light.

Clears the list.

Objects in the list can be chosen by using 3ds Max selection sets.

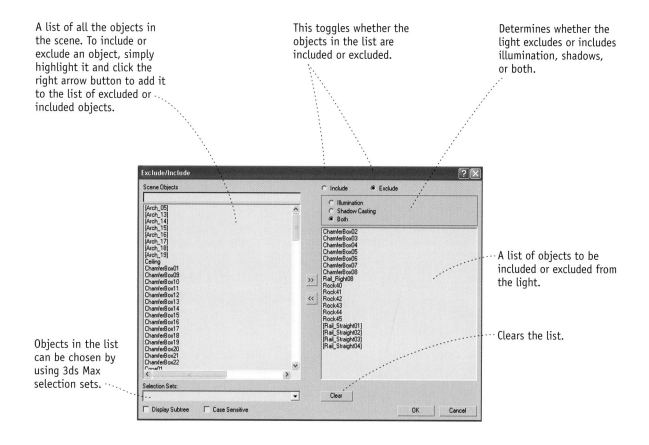

Lighting a Scene

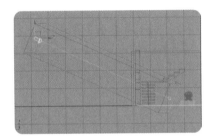

1 Open the scene Museum_start.max. This is a simple scene set in the corner of a museum.

2 Start by creating the light from the sun. Create a Target Direct light and place it outside the room.

3 Give the light a slightly yellowish hue and adjust the directional parameters so that the light falls just across the windows.

4 Render a test. The light is creating highlights on the floor, but the beams of light are not visible.

5 Select the Direct light and add a Volume Light effect to it.

6 A quick render test shows the default values are too strong.

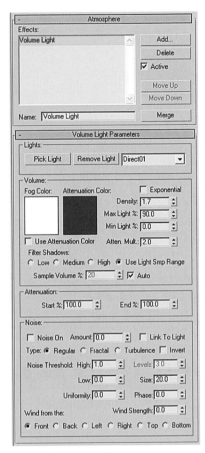

7 Using the light's Atmospheres & Effects rollout, click Setup to open the volume light's controls. Reduce the Density parameter to about 1.7.

8 Another render test shows a more-desirable result.

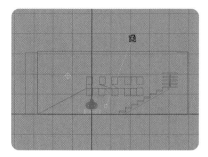

9 Now let's create the main room lighting. Create an omni light in the room at about ceiling height.

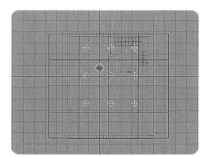

10 Choose Edit → Clone to instance this light eight times. Arrange the lights in a 3 × 3 array above the room.

11 A lighting test shows way too much light in the room.

12 Because we instanced the omni lights, changes to one light will affect all the lights. Select one of the omni lights and reduce the light multiplier to 0.5. Adjust the far attenuation to about 450. This will make each light affect only a small area. Turn on Depth Mapped shadows for the lights as well.

13 A render test shows a better light intensity, but the shadows under the stairs are dark.

14 Select an omni light. Adjust the color to dark gray, and density to 0.5.

15 The shadows look better, but they're a bit too sharp.

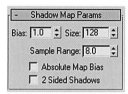

16 Soften the shadows by reducing the Size to 128 and the Sample range to 8.0.

17 A render test shows the shadows are softer. The sculpture, however, is a little dark.

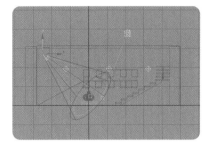

18 Create a target spot and aim it at the sculpture from the direction of the camera. Turn on shadows for this light.

21 This will allow the spot-light to affect only the sculpture and the base. Adjust the light so that the highlights pop on the sculpture but it still looks natural.

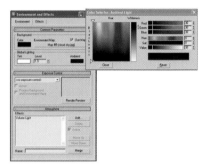

22 Some areas are still dark. Ambient lighting will lighten up some of the dark areas and create the illusion of bounce lighting. Choose Rendering → Environment and adjust the ambient lighting so that it is dark gray.

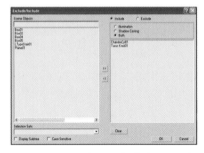

19 A render rest shows the spotlight is affecting all of the scene. Let's limit the light to just the sculpture.

20 Press the Exclude button in the light to bring up the Exclude/Include window. Select the Include radio button along the top of the window. Select ChamferCyl01 and TorusKnot01 and move them to the right-hand side.

23 The scene is nearly complete. Continue to adjust the lights and finalize the scene.

5

Rendering

Rendering is the process whereby your 3ds Max scenes come together into an image. Just as you print film in the darkroom, you truly create an image by rendering it. Creating good renders involves knowing a little bit about the technology behind the scenes, such as the way lights and cameras interact, as well as the way 3ds Max and mental ray smooth and antialias images. Although knowing the technology can get you to the point where you can render almost anything, it's your artist's eye that puts this knowledge to use and makes the difference between a good image and a truly great one.

Renderers

3ds Max has two basic renderers that come with the software: the scanline renderer and mental ray. The type of renderer is selected by using the Assign Renderer rollout of the Render Scene dialog box.

3ds Max's scanline renderer is a fast and robust rendering solution. It produces excellent images and can create advanced effects such as radiosity for architectural and design applications. Mental ray is an industry standard renderer that is used by various other packages. It provides advanced lighting simulations to create global illumination and caustics. Most 3ds Max lights, cameras, and materials will work with both renderers, though each renderer has its own set of tools for those areas that don't overlap.

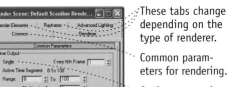

Render Scene Brings up the Render Scene window

Quick Render Renders the scene by using the current settings

Render Type Allows you to render the view, selected objects, regions, and more

ActiveShade Renders the scene in the ActiveShade window, which allows for interactive rendering

Rendering can be started by using the render icons on the main toolbar.

Render Scene Window

Much of the rendering process in 3ds Max is controlled in the Render Scene window (choose Rendering → Render). This window has several tabs. The first is a Common panel that you can use to specify the size and format of the render, the filenames, and other options. It also lets you assign the renderer. The Renderer tab is unique to the type of renderer selected. Other tabs will also appear, depending on the type of renderer selected.

The renderer is assigned by using the Assign Renderer rollout. Clicking the icon to the right of the renderer allows you to assign a new one. Different renderers can be used for production renders, the Material Editor, and ActiveShade.

When a single image is rendered, the result shows up in the Rendered Frame window. This window has options to save the image as well as to view individual RGB and alpha channels.

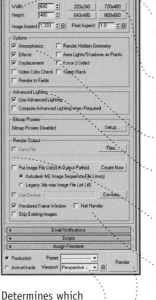

These tabs change depending on the type of renderer.

Common parameters for rendering.

Options to render single, multiple, or specific frames.

Parameters to control the size and aspect ratio of the final output.

Right-clicking these test buttons allows you to set presets.

Various options for rendering.

Turns on advanced lighting in the scanline renderer.

Selects the output filename and file type.

Enabling this check box brings up the Network Render dialog box.

Determines which viewport is rendered.

Renders the scene.

ActiveShade Window

ActiveShade provides interactive rendering for 3ds Max. ActiveShade updates the render as parameters such as lighting and materials are changed. A floating ActiveShade window can be created by using the ActiveShade icon on the main toolbar. Viewports also have an option to be displayed as ActiveShade. You can drag and drop materials from the Material Editor to an ActiveShade window as you can with other viewports.

ActiveShade does have a few limitations. Only one ActiveShade window can be active at a time. Changes to geometry will not update in the ActiveShade window, and it will not render atmospheric effects, rendering effects, or raytraced shadows.

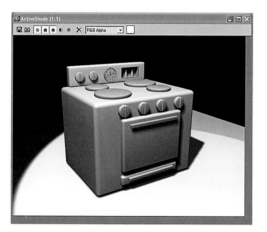
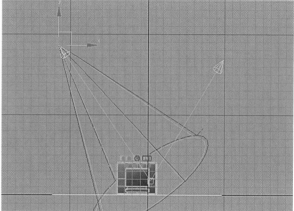

ActiveShade interactively renders a scene.

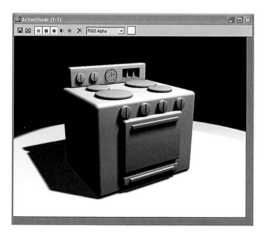
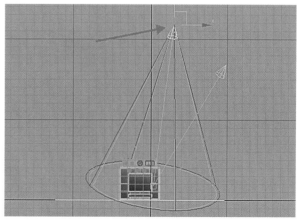

Moving the light in the viewport updates the render.

Object Properties

Each object in the scene has object properties applied to it. Some of these options determine how the object appears in the scene, but they also control how the object is rendered. The Object Properties panel is accessed by choosing Edit → Object Properties, or by right-clicking an object or objects and selecting Object Properties from the object's quadmenu.

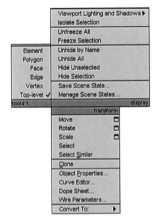

Right-clicking over an object brings up a quadmenu where Object Properties can be selected.

Options for advanced lighting, such as radiosity

Options for mental ray

The name of the object and geometry data

Options to hide or freeze the object

Options to control how the object renders

Options to control how the object is displayed in the viewport

Assigns an object ID for use in render effects

Options for motion blur

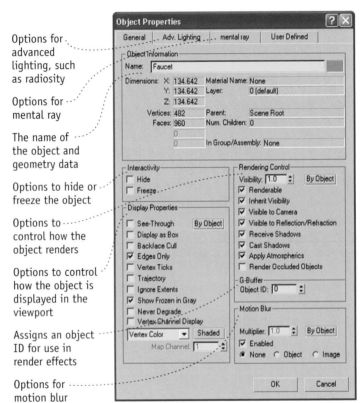

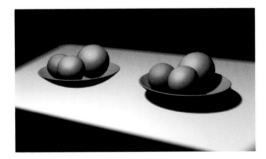

Objects can be set so they cast no shadows.

Visibility affects the transparency of the object, both in the viewport and when rendered.

Cameras

Cameras in 3ds Max are similar to real-world cameras. In addition to controlling what you see through viewports, they allow you to take virtual photographs, or renders, of a scene. Cameras in 3ds Max have controls such as focal length and aperture as well as f-stop and shutter speed for creating effects such as depth of field and motion blur. 3ds Max cameras, however, don't use film, so shutter speed and f-stop do nothing to affect the exposure of the image.

Types of Cameras

Although all cameras in 3ds Max share the same sets of attributes, you'll see two types of cameras listed when you choose Create → Cameras or select the Cameras tab from the Create panel. These are Free Camera and Target Camera; the only difference between these cameras is that the target camera is aimed at a target object.

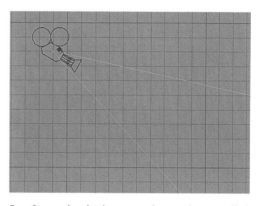

Free Camera is a basic camera that can be controlled by using translation and rotation.

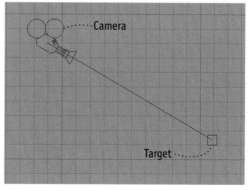

Target Camera always points to the target. This makes positioning the camera simply a matter of translating the camera and the aim point, rather than rotating the camera. This can be useful when the camera is following a moving object. If the aim point follows the object, the camera will too.

Focal Length

The **focal length** of a lens determines the distance it takes for the
lens to focus the image to a point.
The focal length of a lens determines how much of the scene can
be focused, which is called the
field of view (FOV). In 3ds Max,
these two parameters are directly
linked: as the Lens option increases,
the FOV option decreases.

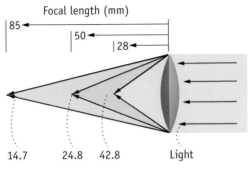

Focal length (mm)

Angle of view (degrees)

The closer the focal point
is to the lens, the wider the
angle of view.

Focal length and angle of view are set by
using the camera's Parameters rollout.
This is also where you set clipping planes.

Focal length 15mm, angle of view 100.3.
An extremely short focal length creates
a fish-eye effect.

Focal length 28mm, angle of view 42.8.
A standard wide-angle lens reduces
this effect.

Focal length 50mm, angle of view 24.7.
A 50mm lens is one of the most common
and is good for most general applications.

Focal length 135mm, angle of view 9.3.
Longer lenses can be good for portraits,
but at very long lengths, the lens might
flatten the scene too much.

Shorter focal lengths mean that objects must be closer to the camera to fill the
field of view. Extremely short focal lengths can distort the perspective of a scene,
and long ones tend to flatten it.

Clipping Planes

Clipping planes define the distances over which the camera will work. This is toggled on by using the Clip Manually option. Clipping planes can, however, be used for various tasks, such as dividing a scene into layers for rendering.

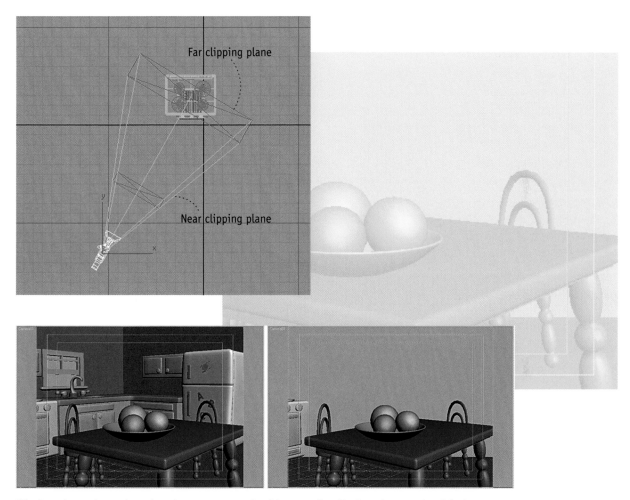

Clipping planes determine what the camera sees. In this case, the clipping plane on the right is set to see only the front part of the set.

You might also want to adjust a clipping plane manually when you are modeling. For example, you might need to work on part of a model in wireframe without being distracted by all the vertices on the back side of the model. By setting the clipping plane close to the working plane, you can hide the far side of the model.

Depth of Field

Depth of field simulates how a real-world camera focuses. Focus is important in cameras because it allows the photographer to guide the viewer's eye to the important parts of the scene. Cameras tend to focus objects in a range of distances. A low depth of field means the range is narrow; fewer parts of the scene will be in focus. Conversely, the higher the depth of field, the more of the scene will be in focus.

3ds Max has several ways to create depth of field, depending on the renderer used. The scanline renderer has Depth Of Field as a multi-pass effect or as a rendering effect. Mental ray has its own tools available in the Render Scene dialog box.

Multi-Pass Effect

The multi-pass Depth Of Field effect is created by toggling on the effect in the camera's Parameters rollout. The actual parameters for the effect are located in the Depth Of Field Parameters rollout. Multi-pass effects are created by rendering the scene in several passes and then averaging the results. These effects can also be previewed in viewports. The downside of using multi-pass effects is that they can slow rendering significantly, because each pass requires that each frame be completely rendered (so 12 passes will render 12 times as slow).

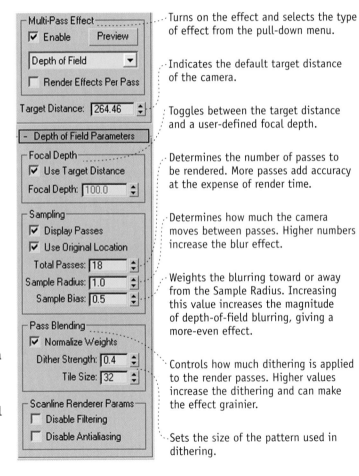

Turns on the effect and selects the type of effect from the pull-down menu.

Indicates the default target distance of the camera.

Toggles between the target distance and a user-defined focal depth.

Determines the number of passes to be rendered. More passes add accuracy at the expense of render time.

Determines how much the camera moves between passes. Higher numbers increase the blur effect.

Weights the blurring toward or away from the Sample Radius. Increasing this value increases the magnitude of depth-of-field blurring, giving a more-even effect.

Controls how much dithering is applied to the render passes. Higher values increase the dithering and can make the effect grainier.

Sets the size of the pattern used in dithering.

 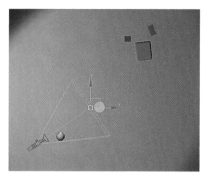

When the camera target is on the cylinder, depth of field is focused on the cylinder.

 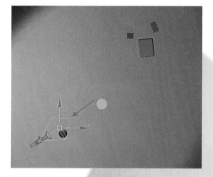

When the camera target is on the sphere, depth of field is focused on the sphere.

When the Sample Radius is increased, the blur increases. With a high degree of blur, the number of samples should be increased to eliminate sampling effects.

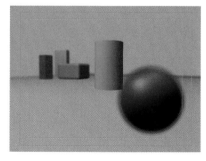

Multi-pass effects can be previewed in viewports.

Depth Of Field Render Effect

The Depth Of Field render effect is applied by choosing Rendering → Effects and adding the Depth Of Field effect to the Effects list. Render effects are post-processing effects, so the scene is rendered by the scanline renderer before the effect is applied. Depth Of Field works by calculating the depth of each pixel in the rendered scene, and then dividing the scene into foreground, background, and in-focus pixels. The foreground and background images are then blurred, and the final image is composited from the processed originals.

Adds and deletes effects from the list

Provides tools to preview the effect as the parameters are changed

Picks the camera to be used for the Depth Of Field effect

Selects an object to be used as the focal point or the camera's target distance

Determines the horizontal and vertical blur

Determines which part of the scene will remain in focus

Determines how quickly the camera loses focus

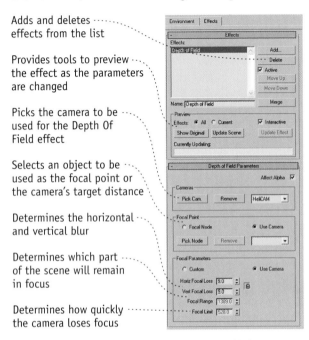

Render Effects window with Depth Of Field applied

Depth Of Field rendered as a render effect

mental ray Depth of Field

Depth of field in mental ray is much more precise. It is similar to how depth of field is calculated in a real camera, in that mental ray uses an f-stop parameter to control the amount of blurring. Setting up depth of field is similar to the multi-pass effect; the camera's target distance determines the focal plane of the camera.

In mental ray, motion blur is configured by selecting the Depth Of Field (mental ray) option in the Multi-Pass effect. When this is selected, the Depth Of Field parameters give you one option to set the f-stop. The f-stop parameter controls the amount of blurring at distances away from the focal plane. In a real-world camera, the f-stop measures the size of the lens's aperture. The lower the f-stop value, the larger the aperture and the more blurring. Mental ray works the same: lower numbers enhance the effect; higher numbers attenuate it.

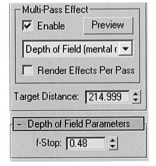

Depth of field for mental ray is controlled by using an f-stop parameter.

Motion Blur

Another camera effect is **motion blur**. In the real world, it takes time to expose a frame of film. If the subject moves during this exposure time, the resulting image is blurred. In 3ds Max, there is no such thing as film speed, so motion blur has to be simulated. This is done in several ways, depending on the renderer. 3ds Max's scanline renderer has three types of motion blur: Image, Object, and Multi-Pass.

Object and Image motion blur are configured on a per-object basis by using the Object Properties panel. Select an object or objects and right-click to produce a quadmenu, which will have an Object Properties option. After you access the Object Properties panel, you can enable motion blur as well as choose the type of motion blur for the objects.

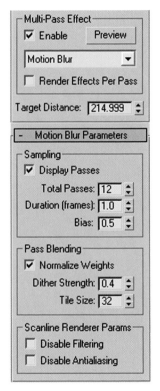

The Motion Blur options in the Object Properties panel. The type of motion blur can be selected, and a multiplier can be set to enhance or dilute the effect for the object.

Image motion blur is a post-render process that simply blurs the pixels of the scene. It renders quickly, but the results are not completely accurate. It does not perform well with overlapping objects, objects that change shape, or reflections.

Image motion blur is also configured in the Render Scene dialog box, via the Renderer tab. The options set the duration of the effect as well as whether transparency will be considered.

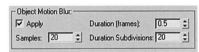

Object motion blur is configured in the Render Scene dialog box, via the Renderer tab. The options set the duration of the effect as well as the number of samples.

Multi-Pass motion blur is a camera effect and is used primarily to simulate the blur caused by a moving camera. It is configured in the camera's Multi-Pass Effect panel.

A low number of samples can cause artifacts (left). A higher number of samples will be smoother but will take longer to render.

Motion Blur in mental ray

Motion blur in mental ray is more robust than 3ds Max's motion blur. Mental ray blurs anything in the scene: shaders, textures, lights, shadows, reflections, refractions, and caustics. Mental ray uses the camera's shutter angle to determine the amount of blur. This is modified on the Render Scene dialog box's Renderer tab, by using the Motion Blur attributes in the Camera Effects rollout:

Shutter Duration Indicates the duration of the shutter in the scene. Higher numbers enhance the effect.

Shutter Offset Offsets the shutter. A zero value starts the shutter at the start of the frame.

Motion Segments Indicates the number of samples to use when calculating blur. Higher numbers are more accurate at the cost of render time.

Time Samples Controls the number of times the material is shaded during each time interval. Rapid changes in reflections or refractions might require a higher Time Samples value.

The Motion Blur option for mental ray can blur such things as shadows and reflections.

Scanline Renderer

3ds Max's scanline renderer is the default renderer for the software and is a good general-purpose renderer. It's the renderer used in most of this book, so you've already had some experience with it. 3ds Max's scanline renderer is also the most tightly integrated renderer available to 3ds Max, and any feature in the renderer can be connected seamlessly with any other feature in 3ds Max. The renderer supports both scanline and raytracing, so only those parts of the scene that need the extra processing power of raytracing receive it.

When 3ds Max Software is the chosen renderer, all its options are controlled through the 3ds Max Software panel in the Render Scene window.

Turns on/off mapping, shadows, reflections, and wireframe

Sets antialiasing style, which determines how edge pixels are smoothed

Performs an additional antialiasing pass on materials

Provides options to control motion blur

Determines the number of times an image reflects

If a color is out of range, decides whether the color is simply clamped to a maximum value or all colors are scaled

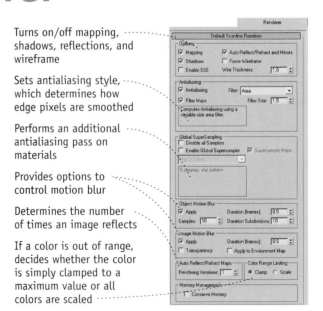

Antialiasing

Antialiasing controls how the renderer smooths and blends jagged-edge pixels. Getting good-looking edges is important to achieving superior-quality renderings, so 3ds Max provides a wide degree of control over the way images can be antialiased.

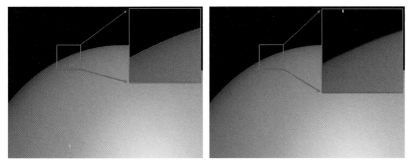

An edge without antialiasing (left) looks jagged, but smooth with antialiasing (right).

Antialiasing is controlled by many different filter types. Each type has its own benefits:

Area Computes antialiasing by using a variable-size area filter.

Blackman A 25-pixel filter that is sharp but without edge enhancement.

Blend A blend between sharp area and Gaussian soften filters.

Catmull-Rom A 25-pixel reconstruction filter with a slight edge-enhancement effect.

Cook Variable A general-purpose filter. Values of 1 to 2.5 are sharp; higher values blur the image.

Cubic A 25-pixel blurring filter based on a cubic spline.

Mitchell-Netravali Two-parameter filter; a trade-off of blurring, ringing, and anisotropy. Setting the ringing value higher than 0.5 will impact the alpha channel of the image.

Plate Match/MAX R2 Uses the 3ds Max 2 method (no map filtering) to match camera and screen maps or matte/shadow elements to an unfiltered background image.

Quadratic A 9-pixel blurring filter based on a quadratic spline.

Sharp Quadratic A sharp 9-pixel reconstruction filter.

Soften An adjustable Gaussian softening filter for mild blurring.

Video A 25-pixel blurring filter optimized for video applications.

Raytracer

Raytracing in the scanline renderer allows it to create highly realistic reflections and refractions. Raytracing works by tracing rays of light from the camera throughout the scene. Raytracing is configured in two places. First, the material must be a Raytrace or another type of material with Raytrace maps in the reflection or refraction channels. Second, the renderer must have raytracing enabled.

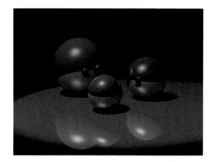

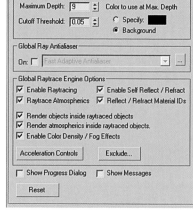

The raytracing tab of the Render Scene window.

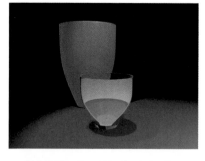

When the depth is set to 0 (top), one object can reflect another, but not much else. Adding more reflections (bottom) allows objects to reflect one another's reflections, adding to the sense of realism.

The number of refractions needed in a scene can add up quickly. We have at least four surfaces to refract (top): two sides of the front of the glass, the front and back of the liquid, and two more sides on the back of the glass. When the depth is set to 2 (middle), only the front part of the glass refracts. Setting it to 4 (bottom) refracts the front of the glass and the liquid, but not the far side of the glass.

Advanced Lighting

Advanced Lighting in the scanline renderer re-creates the way real light scatters through the scene. There are two ways to render advanced lighting effects: by using the Light Tracer or using Radiosity.

The Light Tracer

The Light Tracer creates soft-edged shadows and simulates color bleeding for brightly lit scenes. The Light Tracer does not attempt to create a physically accurate model and can be easier to set up than radiosity. The Light Tracer works well with most lights, but adding a skylight will create softer shadows.

The Light Tracer is activated by using the pull-down menu.

Allows skylights to create soft shadows and scales their intensity.

Determines quality of the render. Higher numbers are better at the cost of rendering speed.

Controls the amount of color bleed.

Controls how many times light will bounce.

Controls quality of the render. Higher numbers render slower.

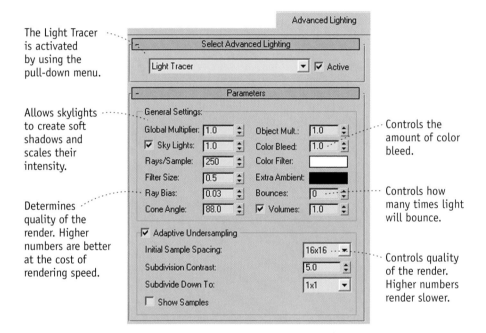

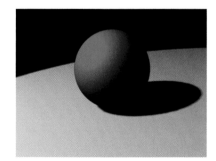

A scene rendered without the Light Tracer.

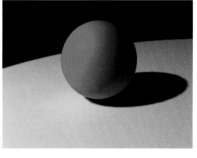

When the Light Tracer is turned on and the number of bounces increased, the light bounces off the floor and illuminates the underside of the sphere. The color of the sphere also bounces, creating a slight green bleed on the floor.

When a skylight is added, it creates softer shadows.

A scene rendered without radiosity

The same scene rendered with radiosity

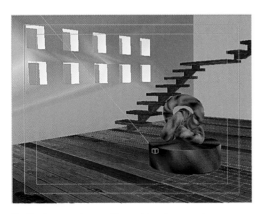

Radiosity can be configured to show up in a viewport for reference.

Radiosity

Radiosity is more complex than the Light Tracer but is also physically accurate. Radiosity scatters light energy throughout the scene, calculating the light intensity for all surfaces in the environment. It is mostly used for architectural renderings, but can be used for animation. Radiosity relies on the photometric lights in 3ds Max to create its effect. Photometric lights are physically accurate, so they must be placed in a physically correct manner.

Radiosity in 3ds Max works by creating a radiosity solution, which calculates a map of how the lighting affects each and every surface of the scene. If the objects in the scene remain still, the solution can be used for any camera angle. This makes it very useful for architectural fly-throughs. If any object in the scene moves, however, then the radiosity solution must be recalculated. This can slow rendering significantly when radiosity is used for animation.

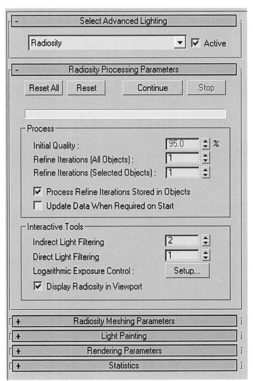

The Radiosity options are also set in the Advanced Lighting panel.

Environment And Effects Panel

The Environment And Effects panel allows you to control such things as the background color, global lighting, exposure, and environmental effects. It is accessed from the main menu by choosing Rendering → Environment.

Background

The background of the scene can be configured by using the Environment map. The background can be a color or a map. The map can be a bitmap or any 3ds Max 2D procedural map. The map can be dragged into the Material Editor as an instance to set mapping styles. The map defaults to screen mapping, which simply stretches the map to fill the screen. You can also map it as a spherical, shrink-wrap, or cylindrical environment.

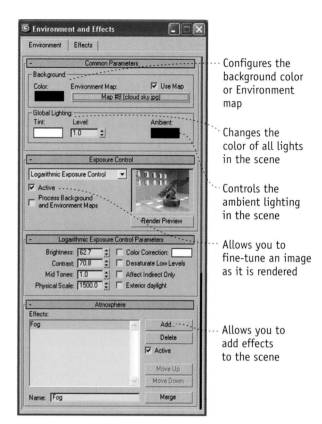

Configures the background color or Environment map

Changes the color of all lights in the scene

Controls the ambient lighting in the scene

Allows you to fine-tune an image as it is rendered

Allows you to add effects to the scene

Screen mapping maps the sky bitmap to the edges of the rendered image.

Spherical, cylindrical, and shrink-wrap environment mapping maps the image to the environment. This allows the camera to be moved. The map must be able to be tiled or else a seam will appear, as in this image.

Exposure Control

Exposure Control is a process that allows you to fine-tune an image as it is rendered. This process can be used for any scanline-rendered scene. It treats the rendered image like a film negative and allows you to adjust exposure much like in a film camera. It can be helpful in matching rendered scenes to live action.

Those who use radiosity will find that exposure control is almost a necessity. Radiosity-rendered scenes can have a wide dynamic range, and exposure control can help bring this wide variation in lighting into a more-useable image.

A radiosity scene rendered without exposure control.

Automatic Exposure Control samples the rendered image and gives good color separation across the entire range of the rendering. It should not be used with animation because it can change the exposure on a per-frame basis.

Linear Exposure Control samples the rendering and uses the average brightness of the scene to remap the RGB values. Linear Exposure Control is best for scenes with a fairly low dynamic range.

Logarithmic Exposure Control uses brightness, contrast, and whether the scene is outdoors in daylight to map physical values to RGB values. Logarithmic Exposure Control is better for scenes with a very high dynamic range.

A Pseudo Color Exposure Control is actually a lighting analysis tool. It maps luminances to pseudo colors that show the brightness of the values being converted.

Environmental Effects

Environmental effects are added by using the Effects rollout at the bottom of the Environment panel. Environmental effects are volumetric effects such as fog and fire. Effects can be stacked in the Effects list, and the effects will be evaluated from bottom to top.

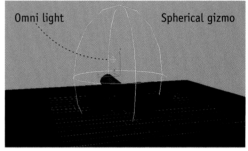

Fire Effect can produce animated fire, smoke, and explosion effects. It can be used for fire, explosion, and nebula-type effects. Fire effects are controlled by gizmo helper objects, which are used to place and scale the effect. Multiple fire effects can be added, so their order in the Effects list becomes important. Fire does not create light or shadows, so it is common to create a light that simulates this part of the effect. The effect is controlled by a gizmo helper, and light is provided by an omni light.

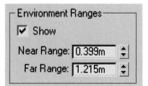

Fog causes objects to fade as they recede from the camera. The Environment Ranges settings in the camera control how the fog is rendered.

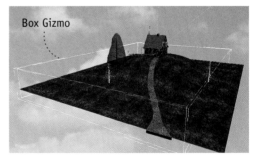

Volume Fog creates fog within a specified volume. It is good for creating misty environments or cloudlike effects. A gizmo helper object specifies the volume for the effect.

mental ray Renderer

Mental ray for 3ds Max is an excellent renderer that has become a standard at many studios around the world. Mental ray can render scenes by using its own scanline algorithm (not to be confused with 3ds Max's default scanline renderer) and it can also raytrace. Mental ray can be more robust than 3ds Max's scanline renderer when it comes to creating highly realistic effects. Global Illumination allows mental ray to simulate the way light bounces off diffuse surfaces, much like Advanced Lighting within the scanline renderer. This can create a much softer and more-realistic scene. Caustics simulate the way light reflects or passes through complex objects and can simulate such materials as glass, water, and reflective metals. Mental ray also has a robust library of material types that can simulate surfaces such as glass, skin, and car paint.

3ds Max has fairly tight integration with mental ray, meaning much of it is invisible to the average user. Shaders, lights, and cameras from 3ds Max transfer over to mental ray with little effort. For additional control, cameras, lights, objects, and shaders all have mental ray attributes that become active when mental ray is used as the renderer. Additional mental ray rendering features, such as Global Illumination and Caustics, can be used on most 3ds Max scenes as well.

Basic controls over the mental ray renderer are located on the Render Scene window's Renderer tab.

Determines the quality of the antialiasing. Higher numbers increase quality.

Determines how much contrast is in the scene on a per-channel basis.

Turns on mental ray's scanline renderer.

Turns on raytracing in mental ray.

Determines the raytrace depth for the renderer as well as for reflections and refractions.

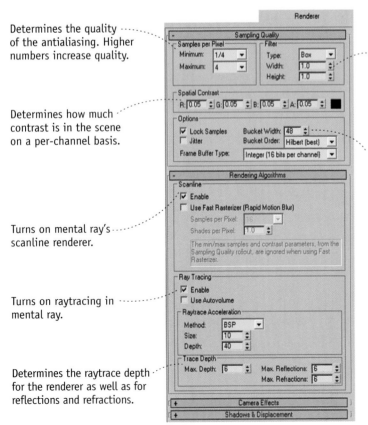

Determines how rendered pixels are filtered for rendering. Different algorithms can be selected with the pull-down.

Determines how much of the image is rendered at a time. Buckets contain render data and can be distributed to other machines during rendering.

Global Illumination

Global illumination is a rendering method used to create highly realistic lighting and shading. It simulates the actual scattering of photons of light around the scene. Although it is computationally expensive, the results are often worth the extra processor time.

Global Illumination is controlled in two places. First, the light must be set up to cast photons; then the renderer must be configured to accept these photons and render the results.

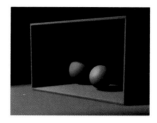

A scene (left) without global illumination and with global illumination (right). Notice how global illumination causes light to bounce within the box.

Derives the number of photons and energy from the settings in the Indirect Lighting tab of the Render Scene window. The spinners in the Global Multipliers box simply multiply these settings.

The amount of energy emitted by the light source. Higher energies create stronger global illumination (or caustics) lighting. This value also depends on the size of the scene. Larger scenes require more energy to get the same lighting effect as a smaller scene.

The actual number of photons emitted when calculating global illumination. More photons create more-accurate results but at the cost of more rendering time.

The actual number of photons emitted when calculating caustics. More photons create more-accurate results but at the cost of more rendering time.

When this is selected, the parameters can be set manually.

The color of the photons. It is usually best to match this color to the light color, but it can be varied for other types of effects.

Allows you to set how quickly the photons lose energy. The default value of 1.0 sets the energy to decay linearly with distance. Higher values limit the energy, and lower values effectively intensify it. Values below 1.0 can create noisy results.

The mental ray attributes for a light

The Light Properties rollout within the Indirect Illumination tab of the Render Scene window. This is where defaults used in Automatic Calculation are set.

Toggles the effect on or off.

Sets the number of photons to use in calculating the global illumination solution. More photons provide a more-accurate solution at the cost of increased render time.

When on, the spinner value sets the size of photons. When off, each photon is calculated to be 1/100 of the radius of the full scene.

When on, uses the spinner value to specify the distance where photons are merged, which can produce smoother results.

Multiplies the effect to increase the contribution of global illumination to the render.

When Global Illumination is used with Final Gather, this can speed the total render time.

The Global Illumination rollout within the Indirect Illumination tab of the mental ray Render Scene window

Photons

There are two main lighting parameters to consider when setting up global illumination: energy and number of photons. **Energy** is the brightness of the light, so more energy produces a brighter global illumination solution. The **number of photons** is similar to a sampling rate and affects the quality of the image. More photons produce more-accurate results but at the cost of additional render time. For physically accurate renders, the number of photons can get incredibly high, into the millions.

Photons = 250. When the number of photons is low, the individual spots of light can be seen.

Photons = 1,000. As the number of photons increases, they start to blend.

Photons = 10,000. Eventually, the photons overlap, and the illumination can be seen. When using just photons to illuminate the scene, it can take millions of photons to completely smooth out the graininess.

Energy

The second major attribute used to calculate global illumination is energy. This is roughly equivalent to a light's brightness. Photons, however, perform only indirect lighting, so increasing energy will increase only the amount of indirect light in the scene. Getting the right illumination requires getting the correct balance between the direct light and indirect light.

Energy is sensitive to the scale of the scene. Larger scenes need much larger energies to get the same amount of lighting as a smaller scene. In addition to the scale of the scene, energy also works in conjunction with the decay value, which determines how quickly the energy dissipates in the scene. A decay of 2 creates an inverse square falloff, which simulates the way a real light illuminates a scene. Lower values create more light; higher values attenuate the light.

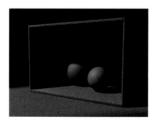

Energy = 4,000, Decay = 2. At low intensities, photons don't do much to provide additional illumination.

Energy = 50,000, Decay = 2. Increasing the photon intensity adds diffuse global illumination to the scene.

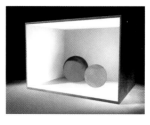

Energy = 250,000, Decay = 2. At very high intensities, the diffuse light from the photons starts to overwhelm the direct lights in the scene.

With the direct light's intensity turned down to 0, the indirect light created strictly by the scene's photons can be seen.

Final Gathering

Final Gathering is used as a finishing tool for Global illumination and can help reduce the need for high numbers of photons. In its simplest sense, it can be used as a blending algorithm, and it smooths and interpolates the light created by the photons to simulate a radiosity solution.

Final Gathering is similar to raytracing, but whereas raytracing traces light rays from the camera's point of view, Global Illumination starts at the light source and traces from there. Final Gathering rays are emitted from a light; when they hit a surface, mental ray calculates the way the rays are scattered, along with their new energies. This process is continued, and the secondary rays of light continue to bounce off other surfaces and so on, creating a soft and realistic lighting of the scene.

Toggles the effect on or off.

Controls quality. A higher number increases the density of the Final Gather sample points.

Controls quality of the final render by controlling the number of rays shown from each light at each Final Gathering step. Low numbers around 100 are good for previews; numbers above 1,000 are good for final rendering. Large numbers can raise render times exponentially.

Sets numbers to control the start and stop of Final Gathering rays (but not Global Illumination photons). Used to limit the reach of indirect light.

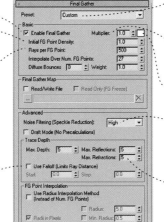

Indicates different presets, which can change the quality of the result.

Multiplies the Final Gather solution. A number greater than 1.0 will brighten the overall lighting of the scene.

Adjusts the overall tint of the Final Gather solution.

Used to eliminate speckles and hot spots in the Final Gathering process. Higher numbers eliminate speckles, but at the cost of accuracy.

Controls the number of times a Final Gathering ray bounces before stopping. Additional values control reflections and refractions.

The Final Gather rollout within the Indirect Illumination tab of the mental ray Render Scene window

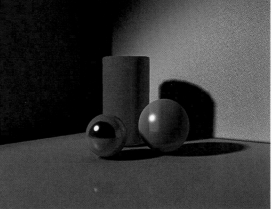

Global Illumination photons are plainly visible in this scene (left); many more photons could be added, but at the cost of rendering time. Final Gathering smooths out the graininess in this scene (right), creating a good final result.

Caustics

Caustics simulates the way light refracts through a complex surface or reflects off it. Caustics are useful in simulating such surfaces as water, glass, and metals. Working with caustics can be a little bit tricky because several variables affect the way the final render looks. The photon intensity and the exponent of the falloff, as well as the distance of the light, number of photons, and the materials of the objects all affect the outcome.

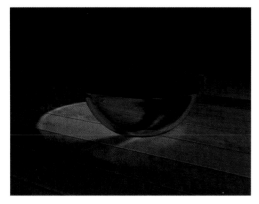

Refractive Caustics simulates the transmission of light through a transparent material.

Reflective Caustics simulates the reflection of light off a surface.

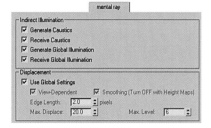

To generate caustics, an object must be enabled in its Objects Properties window.

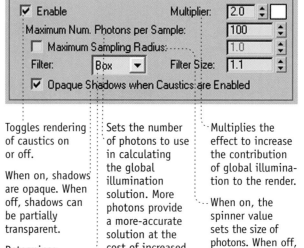

Toggles rendering of caustics on or off.

When on, shadows are opaque. When off, shadows can be partially transparent.

Determines how the caustic photons are filtered.

Sets the number of photons to use in calculating the global illumination solution. More photons provide a more-accurate solution at the cost of increased render time.

Multiplies the effect to increase the contribution of global illumination to the render.

When on, the spinner value sets the size of photons. When off, each photon is calculated to be 1/100 of the radius of the full scene.

The Caustics panel within the Indirect Illumination tab of the mental ray Render Scene window

Energy = 4,000, Decay = 2

Energy = 8,000, Decay = 2

Energy = 16,000, Decay = 2

Energy is probably the most important value when generating caustics. The intensity of caustics pretty much follows the energy of the photons. When the value is too low, the caustics appear faint, but high numbers can easily blow out a render.

The position of the light is another important value to consider. By default, photon intensity decays at the square of the distance from the light. This means that placing the light twice as far away reduces the intensity of the photons by a factor of four. Conversely, moving the light twice as close quadruples the intensity.

Finally, the Decay attribute also plays a factor in how the caustic is generated. This number represents the exponential value at which the light energy decays. Generally, this is kept at the default of 2, which simulates the inverse square law and real-world lighting, but lower numbers can extend the power of the light, and higher numbers will limit it.

Render Elements

The Render Elements tab of the Render Scene window lets you separate out different parts of the render and save them into individual image files. This can be useful when you composite images or work with image-processing or special-effects software. Rendering such elements as shadows or specularity to separate files allows you to adjust their levels inside a compositing package to achieve a more-seamless integration of 3D with live action or other rendered elements.

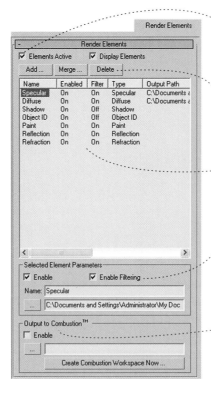

Toggles render elements on or off.

Adds or deletes elements from the list. Merge incorporates the render elements from another 3ds Max scene.

A list of all the elements to be rendered, along with the parameters set for the element.

Parameters to enable the element and enable filtering, as well as set the name and output path.

Outputs to a combustion workspace.

The different types of elements that can be rendered separately within 3ds Max.

The rendered scene.

The Diffuse channel is the color of the objects.

The Specular channel contains just the highlights.

The Shadow channel is the shadows.

The Reflection channel is the reflections.

Backburner

Backburner is an excellent batch and network rendering utility for 3ds Max. It allows you to set up a render farm of multiple machines and manage multiple renders. Backburner is a separate application from 3ds Max and must be started from the Windows Start menu.

Backburner has three main programs: manager, server, and monitor. These are located in the Start menu, under Autodesk/Backburner.

When rendering within 3ds Max, Backburner can be accessed by toggling the Net Render box in the render output section of the Render Scene window. This brings up a window where you can assign the render job to specific servers.

Network rendering is started in three steps:

1. The network manager program is started on one machine.

2. The render servers are started on the rest of the machines.

3. Jobs are submitted.

All machines that are part of the render farm need to have installed a full version of 3ds Max or just the 3ds Max core if the machine is only a render node. Jobs submitted to the network must be submitted from a machine that has a full authorized copy of 3ds Max. In addition, all machines that render must have access to a common network server that can receive the rendered frames.

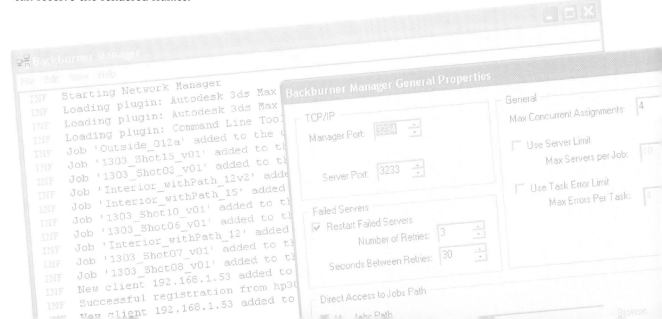

Manager

The manager program controls all render servers in the network. There is typically one manager machine per network. This program must be active and running for network rendering to be active. When the program is run, the manager window will appear on the machine. By choosing Edit → General Settings, you can configure how the manager operates. You can set the number of servers that can be assigned to a job and the number of jobs that can be active at a time. The body of the window will report the status of the rendering process and can be minimized if needed.

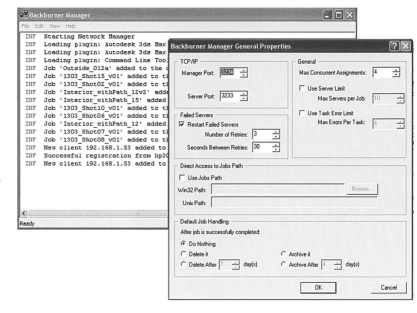

Server

The server controls the rendering process on an individual machine. When the server is assigned a job from the manager, the server launches a copy of 3ds Max and renders the specified frames. The server must be able to see the network drive where the frames will be rendered.

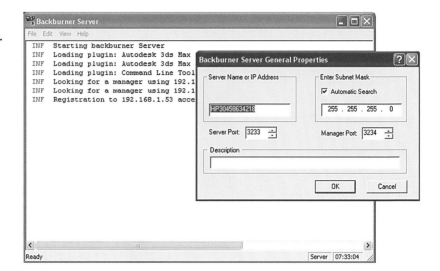

Assigning Jobs

After the manager and server are active, jobs can be assigned to Backburner. This is done via the Render Scene window. When the Net Render box is active, 3ds Max will bring up the Network Job Assignment window when the scene is rendered. The window will first come up with no manager active. Pressing the Connect button will allow you to choose the manager. After this is done, a list of active jobs and servers will appear. You can submit the job to all servers or just selected servers.

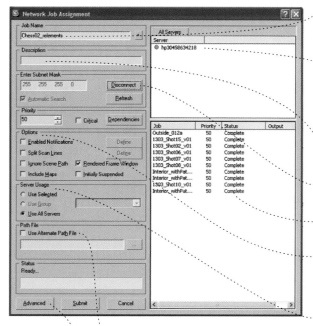

Each job must have a unique name. This defaults to the name of the .max file.

Shows the servers currently active. Servers not rendering jobs will be shown in green. Those busy will be yellow, and those with errors will be red.

In addition to the name, each job can have a text description.

Connects or disconnects to a manager.

A list of jobs currently rendering.

Various options to enable notifications and show rendered scenes in a window, among others.

Assigns the job to selected servers, a user-defined group of servers, or all servers.

Submits the job for network rendering.

Normally, 3ds Max will render to the filename specified in the Render Scene window. This name can be changed here.

Monitor

Render jobs can be monitored and managed by using the Backburner monitor program. This program lists the active jobs and server assignments. It allows you to reassign, reprioritize, and delete jobs.

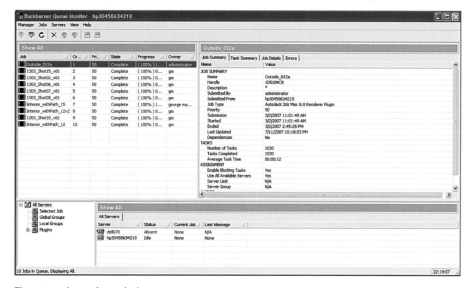

The network monitor window

Rendering Caustics by Using mental ray

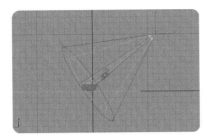

1 Open the file
Caustics_Start.max.
It has a glass bowl on a tabletop
and a single spotlight. Be sure
mental ray is the active renderer.

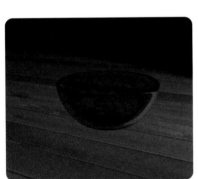

2 Render a test. The render has
no shadows or caustics.

3 Select the spotlight and turn
on shadows.

4 Render a test. The Shadow
map shadows are not accurate
when rendered using the transparent
glass.

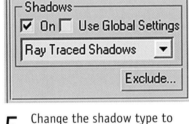

5 Change the shadow type to
raytrace.

6 Render another test. The
shadows are now accurate.

7 Now turn on caustics. This
has to happen in three places:
the renderer, the light, and the
object. First, turn on Caustics
in the Indirect Illumination tab
of the Render Scene window.

8 Select the spotlight and turn
on Indirect Illumination with
the Automatic option.

9 Select the bowl, right-click, and select Object Properties. In the mental ray tab, enable Generate Caustics to make the bowl create caustics.

11 To increase the caustic effect, increase the Energy multiplier in the spotlight to 8.0. Another render test will show more caustics, but the scene could use more.

12 Increase the Energy multiplier to 24.0 and render another test. The effect looks good, but the image looks a little grainy.

10 Render a test. The caustics are not showing up very well.

13 The graininess can be smoothed out with more photons. Increase the Caustic Photons multiplier to 8.0. The render should look smooth.

Rendering Global Illumination by Using mental ray

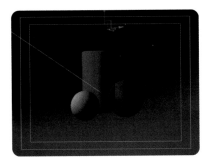

1 Open the file GI_start.max. This image contains a few objects illuminated by a spotlight.

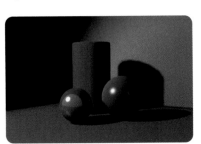

2 Make mental ray the default renderer and render a test. The scene appears fairly dark. Global Illumination will solve this.

3 In the Render Scene window's Indirect Illumination tab, turn on Global Illumination.

4 Select the spotlight. Under the mental ray Indirect Illumination rollout, turn on Manual Settings.

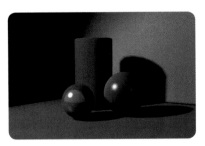

5 Render another test. The effect does not show up well because the photon energy is too low.

6 Select the spotlight and turn the energy up to 50,000. Another render test shows the global illumination effect is present, but the number of photons is too low, creating a spotty effect.

7 Increase the number of photons to 10,000 and render another test. The increased number of photons smoothes out the effect, but it can be smoother.

8 Final Gather can remedy this. On the Render Scene window's Indirect Illumination tab, enable Final Gather.

9 Another render test shows a smoother result. You can continue to adjust values before rendering a final image.

Character Deformations and Rigging

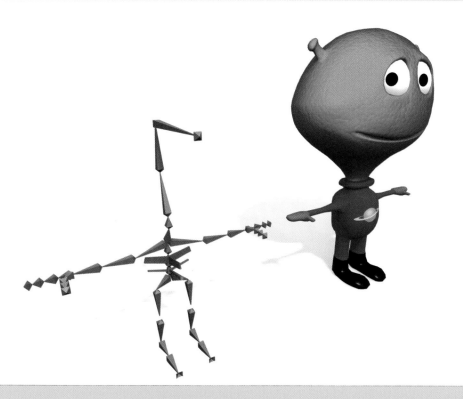

Deformations change the shape of an object. Almost any sort of organic animation—from a fully skinned character to flowers swaying in the breeze—will need deformations of one sort or another. In addition to using deformations for animation tasks, you can use them as modeling tools. Because deformations can reshape a lot of detail quickly, deformers are good choices for global changes to an object.

Rigging is primarily used in character animation to create hierarchical structures called skeletons. **Skeletons** are used as a framework for deforming the character as well as animating it. A good rig builds upon the skeleton to provide additional tools that make the animator's job easier by allowing the character to be quickly posed and manipulated.

Bones

Skeletons in 3ds Max can be constructed from any object but are usually constructed from objects called **bones**, which are tied together in a hierarchy. The skeleton, in turn, is used to deform a mesh via 3ds Max's skinning tools. Although skeletons are used primarily for character animation, they can also be used to create all sorts of other deformations. A garden hose, for example, can easily be deformed by using a series of bones. Bones can also help refine the behavior of hair and clothing.

Bones are used to guide deformations when using the skinning tools. When the bones move, the mesh deforms to match.

Other objects besides bones can be used in skeletons, such as boxes or other bits of geometry.

When building a skeleton, it is always a good idea to study the anatomy of the character or creature you are rigging. Getting the skeleton anatomically correct will make the resulting deformations anatomically correct as well. The bones of this character closely mimic the bones of a real skeleton.

Creating Bones

Bones are created under the Create → Systems → Bones IK Chain menu or under the Systems tab of the Create panel. Bones are drawn by left-clicking to set the anchor point, moving the mouse to set the length, and then left-clicking again to set the end point of the bone and the start of the next bone. Right-clicking ends the operation. When multiple bones are drawn, each new bone is created as a child of the preceding bone, forming a hierarchy. Bone chains can be created with or without inverse kinematics (IK) enabled. When IK is enabled, the IK chain is drawn from the first to the last bone in the chain.

Bones can also have **fins**. These are protrusions on the sides of the bone that can be used to more precisely fit the bone to the mesh.

The Create bones panel

Editing Bones

Bones have a Modify panel where the size of the bone as well as the size and number of fins can be changed. In addition, 3ds Max provides a Bone Tools window (Animation → Bone Tools) to further refine the skeleton.

Remove Bone leaves the hierarchy intact.

Allows you to change the position of the bone's pivot, altering the respective lengths of the bones

Draws new bones, using the standard bone creation tools

Removes the currently selected bone and stretches adjacent bones to match

Deletes the currently selected bone, breaking the hierarchy and the bone chain

Allows you to click on a bone to split it in two

Provides options to turn the bone on, freeze its length, and control its stretch

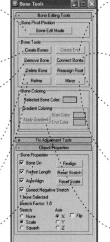

Creates a nub bone at the end of the currently selected bone

Creates a connecting bone between the currently selected bone and another bone

Makes the currently selected bone the root (parent) of the bone structure

Creates mirror copies of selected bones without changing the direction of the bones' scale

Changes the display color of the selected bones

Delete Bone breaks the hierarchy.

The Refine option splits a bone in two.

Inverse Kinematics

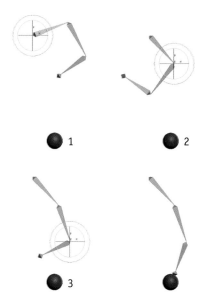

By default, bones in 3ds Max move strictly by rotation. This is called forward **kinematics,** because a series of bones is manipulated from the root bone forward. If a character picks up a cup of coffee, the bones are posed starting at the shoulder and moving forward to the fingertips. Forward kinematics is great for most motions, but it can pose a serious problem whenever a character needs to keep one part of the body stable while the other moves, such as keeping a foot on the ground during a walk or a run.

To get the end of this bone chain to reach the ball by using forward kinematics, all bones in the chain need to be rotated, requiring several steps.

To overcome this limitation, inverse kinematics (IK) can be used. **Inverse kinematics** automatically rotates a chain of bones so that the end points can be positioned by using translation instead of rotation. This is perfect for a character's legs, but also can be used in other areas, such as arms. If a character climbs a ladder, for example, the hands have to remain stable on the rungs while the shoulders move.

Inverse kinematics allows you to position the bones simply by translating the IK handle to the desired location, using one step. The IK solver rotates the bones automatically.

A character's legs are a perfect place to use IK because it allows the hips to move freely while the feet remain firmly planted on the ground.

Working with IK

IK can be applied to a bone chain as it is drawn, or it can be applied afterward by applying an IK solver. Choose Animation → IK Solvers, and then the desired solver. Then select the start and the end bone of the IK chain. 3ds Max has three main IK solvers, plus the ability to do Spline IK. The three main solvers are as follows:

HI solver The History Independent solver uses an IK goal to animate a chain. You animate the goal, and the solver moves the end of the chain to match the position of the goal. This is the preferred solver for most applications.

HD solver The History Dependent solver lets you use sliding joints combined with inverse kinematics. It has controls for spring back, damping, and precedence not found in the HI solver. The solver, however, is history dependent; performance is slower at the end of long animations.

IK Limb solver The IK Limb solver is meant for animating the limbs of characters; for example, the hip to the ankle, or the shoulder to the wrist. Each IK Limb solver affects only two bones, but multiple solvers can be applied to different parts of the same chain.

IK chains are configured by selecting the IK goal and opening the Motion panel.

Selects the IK HI solver or IK Limb solver.

When toggled on, the IK solver is active. When off, the chain is manipulated by using forward kinematics.

Syncs the action of forward and inverse kinematics.

Defines the joints used in the IK chain.

Turns on/off IK interface elements and determines icon size.

Determines at what direction the IK chain points. On a character, the swivel angle controls the direction of the knee or elbow joint.

Allows the swivel angle to point to a target.

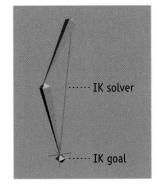

IK solver

IK goal

The IK parameters on the Motion panel

An IK chain is manipulated by moving an IK goal. The IK solver shows which joints are part of the IK chain.

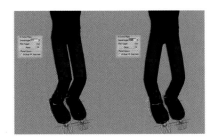

Swivel Angle controls the direction of an IK chain. In this case, it controls the direction of this character's knee.

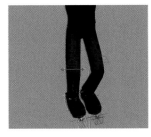

The Select And Manipulate tool can also affect the swivel angle.

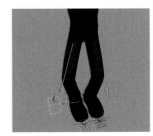

Swivel Angle can also use a target object to control direction.

Using Spline IK

Another way to configure IK is by using Spline IK, which employs a curve to control the bones and their rotations. This is a good choice for manipulating long chains, such as a tail, a trunk, or even a spine.

Spline IK works best with chains that have a lot of short bones. To create a Spline IK chain, draw a bone chain with the Spline IK solver enabled. 3ds Max automatically generates a curve of your choice to fit the chain, plus it gives you the option to create helper objects to manipulate the underlying curve and the chain.

Once created, the Spline IK curve is like any other curve and can be animated by using clusters or blend shapes.

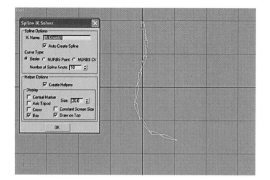

A bone chain drawn with the Spline IK solver enabled allows you to create a Bezier or NURBS curve to control the chain.

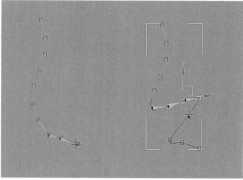

Moving the helper objects deforms the underlying curve and manipulates the bone chain.

Constraints

Constraints are a way to automatically control an object's position, scale, or orientation. Constraints are used in animation as well as in character rigging to provide animators with ways to attach parts of a character's body to other objects or parts of a scene.

Position

In animation, a Position constraint causes one object to move to and follow the position of another object, or the average position of several objects. Position constraints are particularly useful when you want an object to match another object's position while keeping it outside the hierarchy, such as when a character is lifting something.

When the character lifts the ball, the ball is constrained to the palm of the hand. This allows the ball to move with the hand as the hand itself is animated.

LookAt

A LookAt constraint constrains an object's orientation so that the object aims at other objects. In character setup, a typical use of a LookAt constraint is to set up a locator that controls eyeball movement.

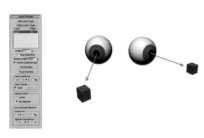

The eyeball is aim-constrained to the locator and rotates to follow it.

Link

A Link constraint allows you to animate the links in a hierarchy. Just as with hierarchical linking, a Link constraint matches the relative position, rotation, and scale of one object to another. The Link constraint, however, can be animated to change the link to a different object at a specific frame. This allows for characters to set down and pick up objects.

The Link constraint allows the ball to be linked to one hand and then another as the ball passes between them.

Orientation

An Orientation constraint matches one object's rotation to another. This can be used in character animation to set up control objects that affect other objects, such as bones within a rig.

The bone is controlled by an Orientation constraint driven by the circle. Rotating the circle swivels the bone.

Surface

A Surface constraint constrains an object to a surface. The types of surfaces that can accept this constraint are limited to surfaces that have UV coordinates, which include parametric surfaces (sphere, cylinder, plane, and so forth) as well as patch, loft, and NURBS objects. The U and V parameters allow the constrained object to be positioned and animated across a surface.

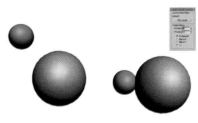

A Surface constraint constrains an object to a surface.

Attachment

An Attachment constraint is similar to a Surface constraint but will work with any polygonal surface. The Attachment constraint works by constraining the pivot point of an object to a specific face on a polygonal object. The constraint shows the face number to be selected along with an offset to fine-tune the position. This constraint works very well for objects that change shape, such as a water surface with waves.

The Attachment constraint constrains an object to a specific polygon on a surface.

Skinning

Skeletons provide the structure of the body, but the skin provides the appearance. Getting the mesh of the character to deform according to the position of the character's skeleton is called **skinning**. Most characters animated in 3ds Max will be skinned in some form, and getting a character's mesh to deform smoothly usually takes a good knowledge of the skinning tools and how they work. The Skin modifier is the most popular way to skin a character, but the Skin Wrap and Physique modifiers also can do the job.

Skin Modifier

The Skin modifier works by using a skeleton or a collection of bones to deform a mesh. Each bone in the skeleton creates an envelope that affects the underlying vertices. Each vertex in the mesh is then weighted to each bone in the skeleton. A bone that completely affects a vertex will be given a weight of 1.0, while bones that do not affect the mesh are given a weight of 0.0. When multiple bones affect a vertex, their weights are somewhere between 1 and 0, but total weights always add up to 1.0.

The Skin modifier also has tools to modify the envelopes as well as tools to assign weights manually and to paint weights. User-defined gizmos can be configured to affect the shape of the mesh depending on the position of a bone.

Vertex selection Tools to select vertices as well as to shrink and grow the selection.

Bones Tools to add and remove bones from the modifier. A bone can also be highlighted in the list so that vertex weights can be set or painted for that bone.

Tools to add or remove cross-sections to the envelopes.

The radius of the envelope as well as tools to control envelope visibility and falloff.

A numeric field to configure the weight of the selected vertices to the highlighted bone.

Enables mirror mode so that weights on one side of the body can be applied to the opposite side.

Decides along which plane the mirroring will occur.

Tools that affect the shape of the mesh depending on the position of a bone.

Include/Exclude Tools to include or exclude the selected vertices from the highlighted bone.

Brings up a spreadsheet-like table where numeric weights can be adjusted.

Uses a brushlike interface to paint skin weights.

Skin tools Brings up the Skin Tools window.

The Skin modifier

Modifying Weights

Vertex weights in 3ds Max can be modified in a number of ways. Envelopes surround each bone and provide the first level of weighting. Vertices that lie within the envelope are weighted to the corresponding bone. Weights can be configured manually or by painting, by using the tools in the Weight Properties rollout.

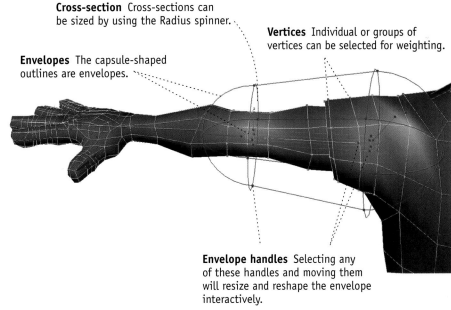

Cross-section Cross-sections can be sized by using the Radius spinner.

Vertices Individual or groups of vertices can be selected for weighting.

Envelopes The capsule-shaped outlines are envelopes.

Envelope handles Selecting any of these handles and moving them will resize and reshape the envelope interactively.

The Skin Weight tool contains a palette of options to set weights for individual vertices or groups of vertices.

Envelopes surround each bone and determine which vertices are affected. Envelopes can be moved and resized. Envelopes can be viewed by selecting the desired bone from the list in the Skin modifier.

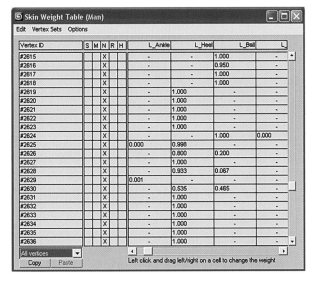

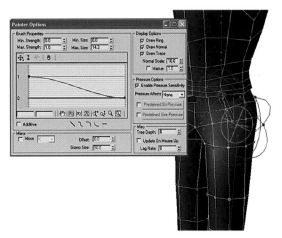

The Skin Weight table is a spreadsheet-like table that allows you to type in numeric weights for vertices.

The Paint Weights tool allows you to paint vertex weights by using a brush.

Using Gizmos

Gizmos affect the shape of the mesh depending on the position of a bone. 3ds Max has three types of gizmos: Joint Angle, Bulge Angle, and Morph Angle. All of the gizmos are set up the same way. The affected bone and vertices are selected, and then the gizmo is added to the list. The joint is then animated through its range of motions, and the gizmos are modified to reshape the mesh according to the joint's angle. The keyframes of the joint's animation are then deleted.

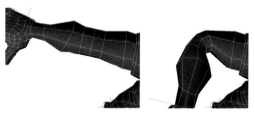

When this elbow joint bends, the mesh deforms improperly.

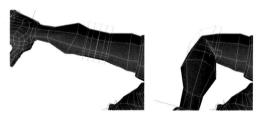

The Joint Angle deformer places a lattice around this joint and gives a proper deformation.

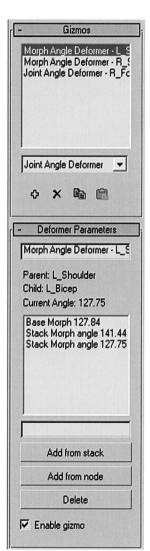

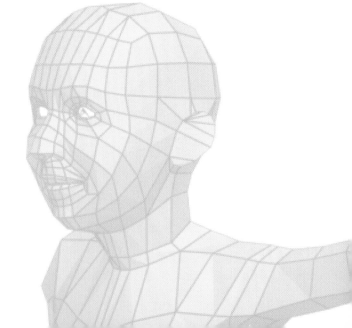

For Joint and Bulge Angle deformers, a lattice is placed around the selected vertices. This lattice can then be reshaped depending on the angle.

The Morph Angle deformer allows you to use 3ds Max's modeling tools to rework the mesh to a precise shape. To accomplish this, add an Edit Mesh or Edit Poly modifier to the top of the stack and reshape the mesh. Use the Add From Stack button to incorporate the new shape.

Skin Wrap Modifier

The Skin Wrap modifier is designed to let a low-resolution mesh deform a higher-resolution mesh. This works well for highly complex characters, because the actual mesh that's deformed is independent of the actual control mesh. This means you can modify the high-resolution mesh and still keep the animation. The low-resolution object doing the deforming is called a **control object**, and the high-resolution object is the **base object**. A base object can be any type of deformable object.

Meshes The low-resolution meshes used as control objects.

Deformations can use either vertices or faces.

The amount of influence a vertex in the control object has on the mesh.

Allows the deformation to be controlled by closest distance rather than specific vertices.

The maximum distance that a vertex on the control mesh can influence the base mesh.

Removes the modifier and replaces it with a Skin modifier that replicates the deformation.

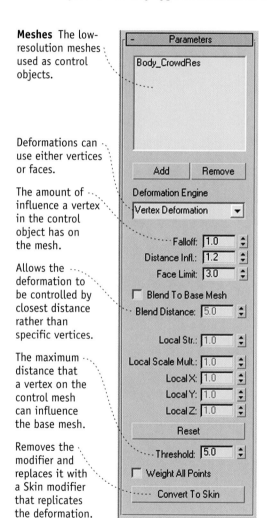

The Skin Wrap modifier

The high-resolution mesh (right) is manipulated by the low-resolution mesh.

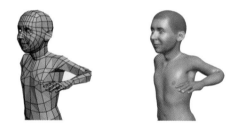

When the low-resolution mesh is changed, the high-resolution mesh matches its movement.

Morphing

Morphs are managed in 3ds Max by using the Morpher modifier. This allows you to change the shape of one object to match that of another. This is a precise way to deform an object, as each target of the Morpher modifier can be modeled by using 3ds Max's modeling tools. Morphs can also combine multiple targets to mix and match deformations.

The big task in configuring morphs is creating the targets. This is primarily a modeling task. The one requirement for blend shape targets is that they all have the same topology as the base object. This is easily accomplished by duplicating the base object (such as a head) and reshaping it to create the appropriate shape (such as a blink or a smile.)

After the targets are created, setting up the morphs is simply a matter of adding the Morpher modifier to the stack and then selecting the targets by using the tools in the modifier. Each target gets a channel, which allows you to set the morph amount for each target.

Morphs work by averaging the X, Y, and Z positions of each individual vertex or CV in the object. When a slider is at 0 percent, the vertex is at the rest position; at 100 percent, it is at the target. Mixing multiple targets averages the positions according to the weights on the sliders.

60 percent   100 percent

Morphs allow you to mix different shapes to create a new result.

Morpher modifier The Morpher modifier is usually placed below the Skin modifier in the stack.

Channels Loaded morph targets appear in this list. Each target has a spinner to set its value. A value of 100 fully morphs to the target. Right-clicking on a channel allows you to load a target from the scene.

Brings up a dialog box where you can select multiple targets from a list of objects.

Reloads the targets. This allows you to reshape targets and update them later.

Sets all channels to zero.

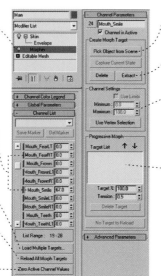

The Morpher modifier

Pick Object Allows you to select morph targets for progressive morphing.

Creates a new mesh representing the shape of the current channel.

Limits Allows you to adjust the minimum and maximum values for a channel. Values can go below 0 and above 100.

Sets up progressive morphing, which animates a mesh through a list of targets as the spinner moves.

Facial Animation Using Morphs

Although morphs can be used for any type of shape animation, by far the most popular application for blend shapes is in facial animation. A modeler creates individual facial poses representing the extreme motions of the individual parts of the face, such as opening the jaw or a smile. By mixing these, you can create an infinite variety of facial expressions.

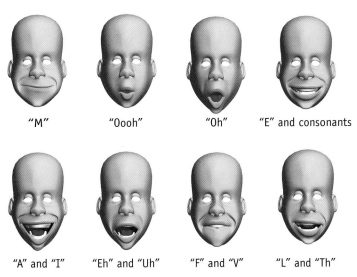

"M"   "Oooh"   "Oh"   "E" and consonants

"A" and "I"   "Eh" and "Uh"   "F" and "V"   "L" and "Th"

Blend shapes called **phonemes** can be created to mimic the basic mouth positions used in dialogue.

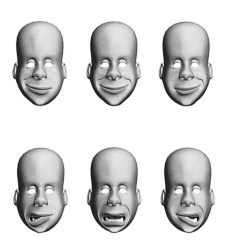

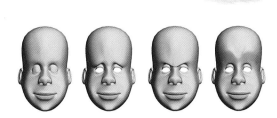

Other blend shapes can be modeled for positions the mouth makes when not speaking, such as a smile. It's always a good idea to create right and left versions of these shapes so that the animator can create asymmetry in the facial expressions.

Shapes for the upper part of the face include blinks and brow positions for emotions such as worry, anger, and surprise. Again, it is a good idea to create left and right versions of these shapes to give the animator more control.

Progressive Morphs

Morphs typically work by moving the vertices of the object from one position to another along a straight line. This default motion works great for many applications, such as facial animation, but can be problematic when morphing an object that needs to move along an arc, such as the joints of a finger or eyelids moving across the round surface of the eyeball. Progressive morphing addresses this problem by allowing a morph to pass through multiple targets, giving you the ability to create **in-between** shapes.

Using a standard morph, the vertices on the finger move directly from the straight to curled targets, creating an improper in-between shape.

Progressive morphing allows for the in-between shape to be specified with an additional target.

Wiring Parameters

3ds Max provides tools that allow you to connect the action of one parameter to another. This is called **wiring** and is useful in character rigging as well as other areas. Wiring allows you to create control panels for characters and areas such as facial animation. It also allows animation along one part of a character to affect others.

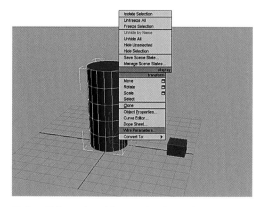

Right-click on the object and select Wire Parameters.

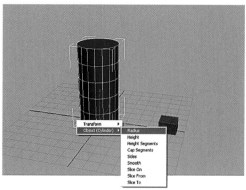

Select the parameter to wire. In this case, the cylinder's radius is selected.

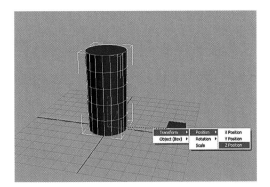

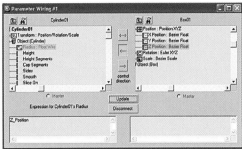

Drag the link to the control object and select the parameter used as the control. In this case, the box's Z position is used to control the radius.

This brings up the Parameter Wiring window, where the parameters and control direction can be set. In addition, expressions can be added.

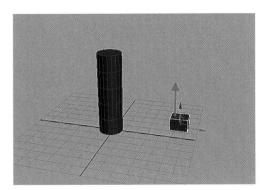

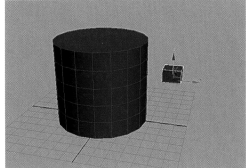

The wiring is complete. When the box is moved along Z, the radius of the cylinder changes to match.

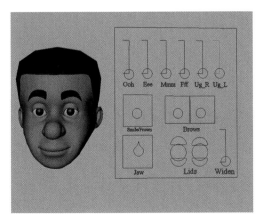

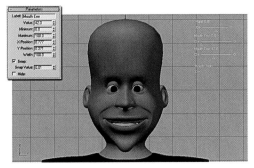

Parameter wiring is used to create control panels, such as this one used to control facial animation.

3ds Max has manipulators, which allow you to create floating sliders in a viewport. These can also be used with parameter wiring to create control panels.

Creating a Skeleton

1 Open the file
AlienSkel_Start.max. This
contains the character created in
Chapter 2. Select the mesh and
freeze it.

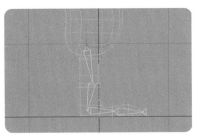

2 In the left viewport, use the
Bone tool (choose Create →
Systems → Bones IK Chain) to draw
four bones representing the thigh,
shin, foot, and toe. Set the width
and height of the bones to 1.0 to
match the scale of the character.

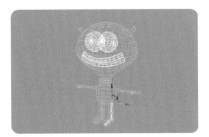

3 In the perspective viewport,
highlight the chain by clicking
the root joint and move it to
position it in the middle of the
left leg. Copy this chain (hold the
Shift key, left-click, and drag) to
make the right leg skeleton.

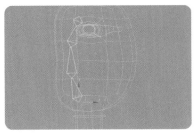

4 In the left viewport, create
a three-joint spine. Follow
the general outline of the back
of the character.

5 In the front viewport, use
Select And Link to link the
legs to the spine.

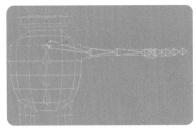

6 In the front viewport, draw the
bones for the right arm, wrist,
and hand. Because this character is
wearing mittens, you don't need
bones for the individual fingers.

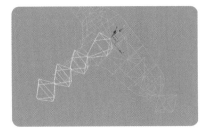

7 Create bones for the thumb.

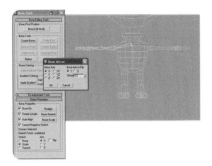

8 Open the Bone Tools window
(choose Animation → Bone
Tools). Select the root joint of the
left arm and mirror this across the
XY-axis to create the right arm.

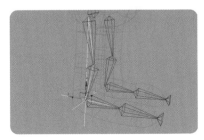

9 Create a neck joint and one
large joint for the head.

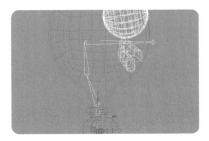

10 Create an IK chain for each
leg. Choose Animation →
IK Solvers → HI Solver, and then
select the root of the left leg
(at the hip) and the left ankle.
Repeat this for the right leg.

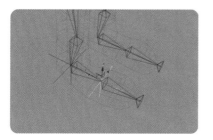

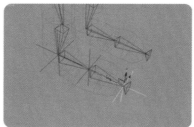

11 To maintain control of the foot, create an IK handle between the ankle and the toe on each leg. This will allow the foot to point at the IK handle rather than rotate with the ankle joint.

12 Select the IK handle of the toe, and make it the child of the leg's IK handle. This will allow you to move the entire foot by grabbing the ankle, and change the angle of the foot by adjusting the handle at the toe.

13 The completed skeleton is ready for skinning.

Skinning a Character

Properly skinning a character is a detailed process. It requires testing the character over a wide range of motions and making sure all the vertices deform properly. This tutorial gives you the broad strokes; the detail work is up to you.

1 Open the file AlienSkin_Start.mb. Select the mesh and apply a Skin modifier (Modifiers → Animation → Skin).

2 Use the Add button in the modifier to add all the bones into the modifier.

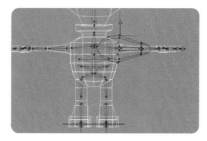

3 Start adjusting the envelopes. Enable the Edit Envelopes button. Select a bone from the list or the viewport and scale the

envelopes so that they fit the character. Vertices will turn red as the envelope affects them.

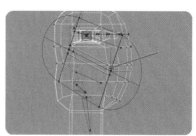

4 The position of the envelope can also be changed by selecting the dots at the end of the bones and moving them.

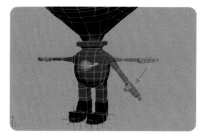

5 To test the weighting on the shoulder, select the L_Bicep bone and rotate it.

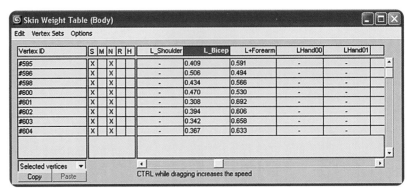

6 You can adjust the weights of individual vertices by enabling the Vertices option, selecting an envelope (in this case, the L_Bicep), and then selecting the vertices.

8 To see how multiple bones affect a set of vertices, click the Weight Table button and use the Weight Table window to adjust the weights.

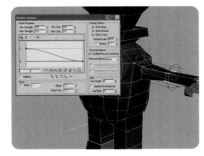

7 Using the Abs. Effect spinner, adjust the weight of the vertices for the selected envelope. Scrubbing the animation will show how the new weight affects the deformation.

9 The Paint Weights tool can give you an interactive way to assign weights.

10 Now you have a basic understanding of the tools used to weight the skin. The rest is just detail work. Continue to use the tools and create test animations to refine the behavior of the skin.

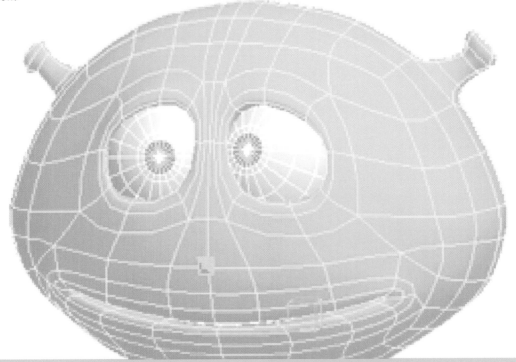

7

Animation

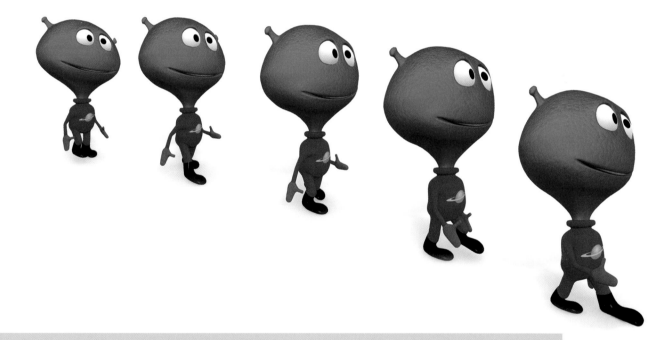

So far, we've been working in the three dimensions of space. Time adds a fourth dimension to your work. Changing an object over time is called **animation**, and animation is what truly brings your scene to life. The way an object moves tells the audience a lot about its size and weight and, for characters, its personality.

3ds Max has a wealth of tools for creating and sculpting motion. Learning how to use the tools, though, is only the first step in the process. An animator must understand how the laws of motion work, as well as how the audience perceives motion. Character animators also have to learn how motion affects a character's personality and mood.

Creating Animation

3ds Max offers a variety of methods for creating animation. Each method has its advantages. Understanding each method will let you decide which approach to take when animating a scene.

Creating keys is the most common way of animating within 3ds Max. A **key** simply records a parameter's value at a given point in time. By changing the value over time, you create motion and animation. Keys allow you a wide degree of control over every parameter of an object, from its position to its color, and just about everything else. To edit keys, you use the Curve Editor and the Dope Sheet. Both allow you to control timing precisely.

Attributes such as position, rotation, and scale can be animated to control how an object moves through space.

Any attribute attached to an object can be animated, such as this object's color.

Parametric animation uses a set of user-defined parameters to create motion.

Constraints can match the motion of one object to another, such as this car to the path defined by a curve.

Using Controllers

Controllers are the heart of animation in 3ds Max. Everything that can be animated in 3ds Max is handled by a controller. A **controller** is a motion plug-in that handles the motion data created through animation. Constraints, as described in the previous chapter, are also driven by controllers. Some controllers can be keyframed, others use scripts or mathematical formulas, and others create motion based on user-defined parameters. Much like modifiers used in modeling, controllers can be stacked in a list so that complex motions and animations can be achieved. Much like with modifiers on the modifier stack,controllers can also be copied and pasted to copy animation. Controllers can also be instanced so that changes in the animation of one object affect another.

Controllers are automatically added to a parameter when it is keyframed. These parameters are typically the parameters involved with transformations (position, rotate, scale) but can be any animatable parameter. Controllers can also be added to existing objects to modify the way the objects are animated. Controllers are found under the Animation option of the main toolbar. They can also be assigned and managed in the Curve Editor, the Dope Sheet, and the Motion panel.

Keyframe Controllers

The most common type of controller manages the keyframing of an object's parameters. These keyframes show up on the time slider as well as in the Curve Editor and Dope Sheet, where they can be edited.

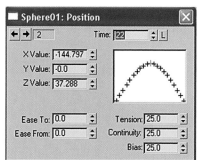

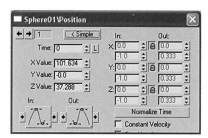

The Bezier float controller is the most common of the controllers. It allows motion to be keyframed with the in-betweens defined by a Bezier curve. Linear controllers (not shown) interpolate the animation linearly, creating a straight line in between keyframes.

TCB controllers produce curve-based animation but do not use Bezier tangents or adjustable tangent handles. These controllers use fields to adjust the Tension, Continuity, and Bias of the animation. The TCB controller creates smoother rotations but does not allow for curve editing.

Parametric Controllers

Some controllers use a set of user-defined parameters to create motion. These controllers do not need keyframes to operate; after the parameters are set, the animation proceeds on its own.

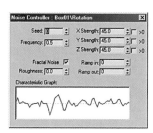

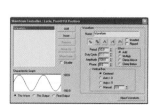

The Audio controller converts the amplitude of a sound file or real-time sound wave to values that can drive the animation of almost any parameter. This is great for syncing animation to sound.

The Noise controller uses random noise to create animation. The strength and frequency of the noise can be adjusted.

The Spring controller adds springlike dynamic effects to any point or object position, to create secondary motion. This constraint adds realism to generally static animations.

The Waveform controller creates periodic waveforms. This is good for any type of regular animation, such as a blinking light or a pendulum.

Script and Expression Controllers

3ds Max has controllers that allow you to manage the motion of an object by using either expressions or scripts. **Expressions** are mathematical equations that connect the motion of one object to another. **Scripts** are more complex and allow for the inclusion of MAXScript, a programming language native to 3ds Max.

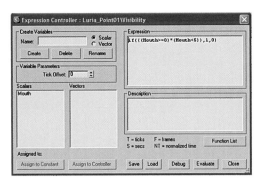

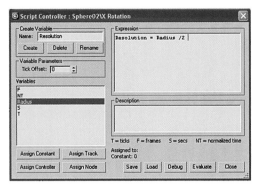

Expressions use mathematical formulas to control animation.

Scripts use MAXScript programming to control animation.

Motion Capture Controller

The Motion Capture controller uses input from an external device to control the animation of an object in real time. The controller can use a number of different input devices such as a mouse, keyboard, joystick, or a MIDIcontroller. After the controller is assigned and the input device is configured, the actual motion is captured by using the Motion Capture utility in the Utilities panel.

The Motion Capture controller allows real-time animation via external devices.

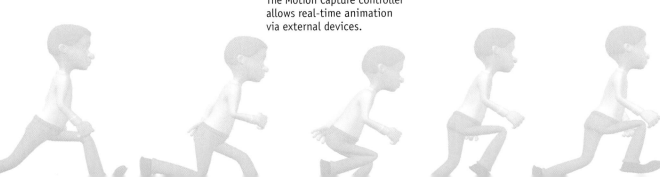

Creating Keys

In 3ds Max, animation is defined by keys, which record parameter changes over time. Almost anything in 3ds Max can be animated, from an object's position in space to its shape and color. There are two main ways of creating keys: Set Key and Auto Key. When either is active, the viewport is bordered in red to let you know that you are keyframing.

Auto Key When this button is activated, any changes to any parameter are keyframed.

Set Key The Set Key button along the bottom of the time slider allows you to manually set a keyframe.

Working with the Time Slider

The time slider allows you to move quickly from one frame to the next in order to set keyframes or scrub through your animation. The slider is a horizontal bar, divided into frames.

Keys Each key in the timeline hows up as a box at the keyed frame. Each box is color-coded: red represents a position key, green is rotation, and blue is scale. Gray keys are for nontransform parameters.

Slider Left-clicking and dragging moves the time slider.

Advance Clicking the arrow advances the time by one frame.

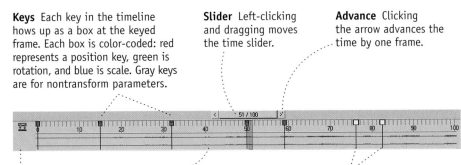

Graph editor Clicking this button brings up a graph editor instead of the time slider.

Sound Sound is imported into 3ds Max. You can then display it by right-clicking in the time slider and choosing sounds from the menu. Visualizing the sound against your keys helps the animation process.

Selecting keys Left-click and drag to select multiple keys. You can then left-click and drag these along the timeline.

Right-clicking a key allows you to bring up a menu from which you can edit and filter keys as well as set playback options.

After keyframes for a particular scene are set, you can play back the animation. You can play back directly in a viewport simply by clicking the Play button, located toward the bottom-right corner of the 3ds Max interface.

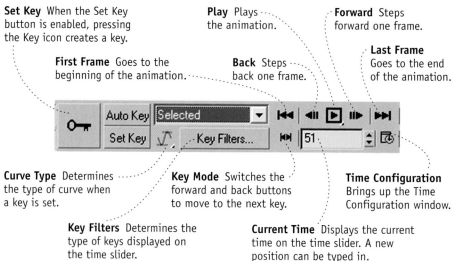

Set Key When the Set Key button is enabled, pressing the Key icon creates a key.

Play Plays the animation.

Forward Steps forward one frame.

First Frame Goes to the beginning of the animation.

Back Steps back one frame.

Last Frame Goes to the end of the animation.

Curve Type Determines the type of curve when a key is set.

Key Mode Switches the forward and back buttons to move to the next key.

Time Configuration Brings up the Time Configuration window.

Key Filters Determines the type of keys displayed on the time slider.

Current Time Displays the current time on the time slider. A new position can be typed in.

Time Configuration lets you define the frame rate, time display, real-time playback, and the length of the animation.

Make Preview

Even on the fastest workstation, complex scenes often do not play back in a viewport in real time. This is when you need to use 3ds Max's Make Preview feature (choose Animation → Make Preview), which steps through the animation and renders a small movie file to disk that actually can be played back in real time.

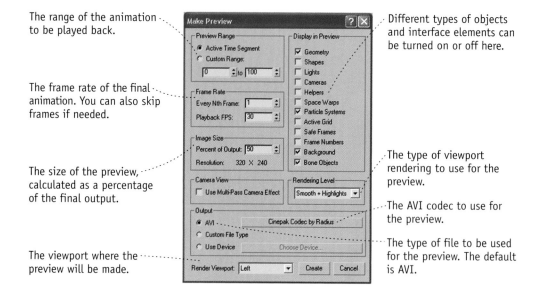

The range of the animation to be played back.

Different types of objects and interface elements can be turned on or off here.

The frame rate of the final animation. You can also skip frames if needed.

The size of the preview, calculated as a percentage of the final output.

The type of viewport rendering to use for the preview.

The AVI codec to use for the preview.

The type of file to be used for the preview. The default is AVI.

The viewport where the preview will be made.

Using the Motion Panel

The **Motion panel** is a place where you can assign controllers, set keyframes, and manage motion. The panel can be considered a close cousin of the modifier stack. Whereas the modifier stack allows you to add modifiers to change the shape or character of an object, the Motion panel allows you to configure and animate controllers that shape the character of the object's motion.

Parameter Mode

Parameter mode displays an object's controllers and allows you to change or modify them. You can also set and manage keys for keyframable controllers and adjust parameters for other types of controllers.

Chooses between parameter and trajectory mode.

Assigns a controller to the selected item in the controller list.

Allows you to create and delete keys.

Key number Each key is assigned a number. Clicking the right- or left-arrow button steps through the keys.

The actual time of the key.

The value of the key.

In/Out curves The curve type for the space before and after the current key.

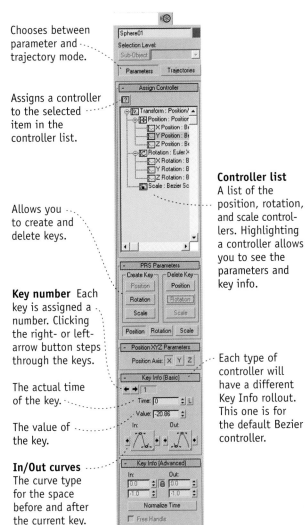

Controller list A list of the position, rotation, and scale controllers. Highlighting a controller allows you to see the parameters and key info.

Each type of controller will have a different Key Info rollout. This one is for the default Bezier controller.

Trajectory Mode

Trajectory mode displays an object's trajectory through a scene. This can be very helpful in visualizing an object's motion. The panel allows you to add and delete keys as well as move, rotate, and scale keys. You can convert a spline path to a trajectory or create a trajectory from an existing spline path.

Enabling this option allows you to add or delete keyframes.

Adds or deletes a key at the current frame.

Allows you to create a spline path from an existing trajectory or to create a trajectory from a spline.

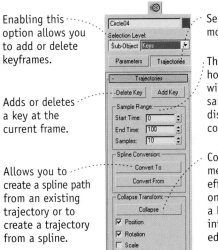

Selects trajectory mode.

This determines how the trajectory will be time-sampled for display and spline conversion.

Collapses a parametric controller effect, such as one generated by a Path constraint, into standard, editable keys.

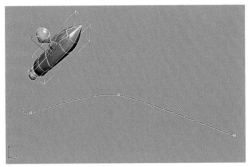

This spaceship is following a trajectory.

Using Track View

Once set, keys can be edited to fine-tune the look and feel of the scene. Simple editing can be done on the timeline by selecting and moving keys or right-clicking them to bring up their controller properties. Keys can also be edited in the Motion panel as well as in the Curve Editor and Dope Sheet.

Track View is the interface where you can edit animation for multiple objects as well as assign and edit controllers. The window has two modes: the Curve Editor and the Dope Sheet.

Provides options to assign controllers as well as copy and paste them.

Provides tools to add and manipulate keys. Groups of keys can be scaled or slid.

Provides options to control navigation and interactivity.

Provides access to Pan and Zoom tools.

Provides access to tools for selecting, managing, and randomizing keys.

Provides options to limit the amount of data displayed.

Switches between the Curve Editor and the Dope Sheet.

Adds a visibility and/or note track to the selected object.

Allows you to apply an ease or a multiplier curve.

Tangent Types These buttons change the type of tangent on the selected keys.

Filters Filters out unwanted controllers in the controller list.

Controller list Lists controllers available for editing.

Selected controllers Selected controllers are highlighted, and their keys show up in the editing window.

Curve Tangents Tangents can be adjusted by using the Bezier handles.

Animation Curves Animation curves appear for the selected controllers. These are color-coded. Red curves represent position, green represents rotation, and blue represents scale.

Select By Name Selects controllers by name.

Track Sets Allows you to create named sets of controllers for easy recall.

Pan Pans the editing window.

Zoom Interactive zoom of the editing window.

Keys Keys are represented as small boxes on the animation curves. Selecting a key allows you to move it or change its tangent.

Zoom controller Zooms the controller list to the selected controllers.

Time Slider Scrubs through the scene.

Zoom Extents Zooms to the horizontal or vertical extents of the animation curves.

Zoom Selected Zooms to a user-defined area.

Track View in Curve Editor mode

Curve Editor

The Curve Editor displays keyframes as curves. These curves display not only keys, but also the interpolation between keys, giving you complete control over the animation. Each key can be given a tangent type, and if the tangent is a Bezier curve, the shape of the curve can be adjusted.

Working with Curves

Curves define how an object will move. Curve tangents define how the curve is shaped before and after a specific keyframe. By using tangents, you can sculpt the object's motion to create effects such as acceleration and deceleration as well as constant linear motion. Tangents can be applied in either the Curve Editor or the Dope Sheet.

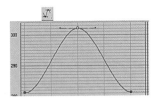

Custom These are the default and use Bezier handles to control the shape of the curve.

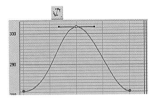

Flat Very much like Bezier curves, but the curves are calculated to eliminate overshoot.

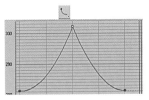

Fast Causes the animation to speed up around the key.

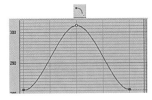

Slow Causes the animation to slow down around the key.

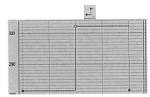

Stepped Simply jumps from one key to the next. Useful for mechanical attributes that are either on or off, such as a switched light.

Linear This tangent offers no change in velocity and is good for objects moving at a constant rate of speed.

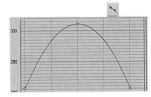

Smooth Creates smooth interpolation through the key without Bezier controls.

Out-of-Range Types

When you create keys for an object, you are creating animation over a specific range of time—from the first key to the last. For those times that lie outside of the keys, you can use Out-of-Range types to define how the animation continues outside of the range defined by the keys. This can be used to create cycles of the keys or just hold the last key. These are found in Track View under Controller → Out-Of-Range Types.

Holds the value of the last key

Cycles the animation from first key to last

Loops the animation

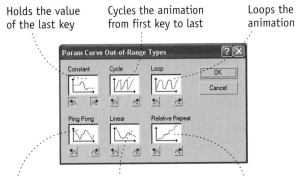

Moves forward and back through the range of keys

Continues the curve at a linear rate depending on the rate at the last key

Cycles with an offset to match the last key to the first

Dope Sheet

The Dope Sheet presents animation as keys set against a horizontal timeline. This window is used primarily to adjust and set timing because you can see all the keys in a scene at once. You can move, scale, copy, paste, and adjust keys individually, in groups, or hierarchically.

Select Tie Selects a range of keys.

Delete Time Deletes keys in the selected range.

Reverse Time Reverses keys in the selected range.

Scale Time Scales the keys in the selected range.

Edit Ranges Creates a mode where you can edit and scale the animation ranges.

Controllers Lists controllers available for editing.

Object key Each object has a master key. Editing this key affects all keys for the object.

Transform key Editing this key affects all transforms for the object.

Keys Keys appear as colored boxes. Selected keys are shown in white.

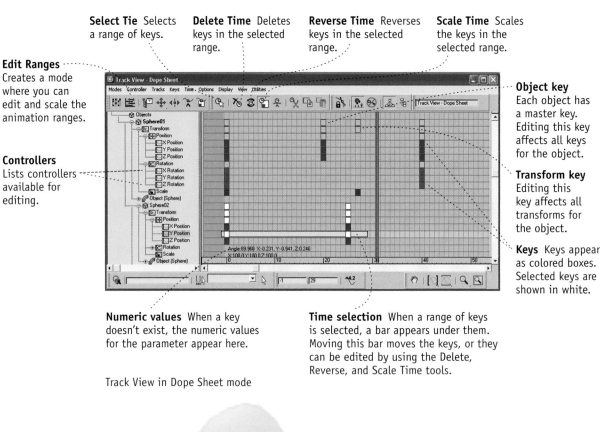

Numeric values When a key doesn't exist, the numeric values for the parameter appear here.

Time selection When a range of keys is selected, a bar appears under them. Moving this bar moves the keys, or they can be edited by using the Delete, Reverse, and Scale Time tools.

Track View in Dope Sheet mode

Animation Layers

Animation layers (Animation → Animation Layers) let you combine multiple animation tracks on the same object. These layers can be turned on and off as you desire to test out different animations or to keep parts of an animation separate. Layers can be mixed by using the Layer Weight parameter.

Enable Anim Layers Creates a new animation layer for the selected object

Layer Weight Adjusts the amount that the selected layer affects the animation

Collapse Layer Collapses the active layer to the one below it

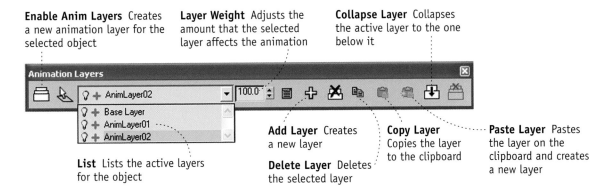

List Lists the active layers for the object

Add Layer Creates a new layer

Delete Layer Deletes the selected layer

Copy Layer Copies the layer to the clipboard

Paste Layer Pastes the layer on the clipboard and creates a new layer

Parameter Collector

The Parameter Collector lets you create rollouts of animatable parameters so that you can find and key parameter sets with a click or two. One of the Parameter Collector's most powerful features is the ability to change all parameters in a collection. One example is in character animation, where you could animate all the fingers in a character's hand so that they all curl simultaneously.

Absolute/Relative Allows multiple edits to be absolute or relative to the given position.

Multiple Edits When this is enabled, you can edit multiple parameters.

Rollouts Parameter sets are stored in user-defined rollouts.

Parameters Parameters appear in a rollout.

Multi Edit Enable When these check boxes are selected, changes to one affect all that are selected.

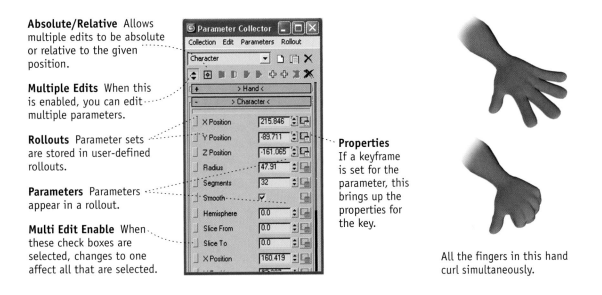

Properties If a keyframe is set for the parameter, this brings up the properties for the key.

All the fingers in this hand curl simultaneously.

Creating a Walk Cycle

1 Open the file `AlienStart.max`. This has a rigged character with a rig similar to the one created in Chapter 6.

2 Start the walk with the legs. Move the time slider to frame 0. Select the Foot control handles at the ankles, and position the feet so they are apart with the right foot forward. Select and move the pelvis so it is halfway between the feet. Rotate the pelvis slightly so the right hip is forward. Set keys for all Foot controls (including the toes) and the Hip control.

3 Move the time slider to frame 6. Turn on Auto Key to make keyframing easier. Select the Hip

control and move it up and forward so the hip is above the right foot. Select the left Foot control, and move it forward and up so the left foot is off the ground at the point where it passes the right leg. Adjust the control at the left toe to point the toe down.

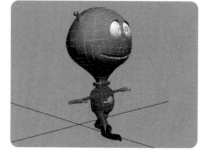

4 Move the time slider to frame 12, and create a mirror pose to that on frame 0, with the left foot forward and the pelvis rotated so the left hip is forward.

5 Repeat the same poses over frames 12–24, making the right foot pass the left at frame 18.

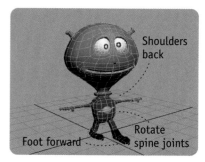

Shoulders back

Foot forward

Rotate spine joints

6 Now set some keys for the spine. As the pelvis rotates to the right, the spine and shoulders rotate to the left. Set keys at frames 0, 12, and 24 to create a balanced pose for the spine.

7 The arms are next. When the right foot is forward, the right hand is back, and vice versa.

8 Finally, the head. Animate rotation on the head so the character is facing forward.

Character Studio

C haracter Studio is a collection of tools that allows for sophisticated animation of characters in 3ds Max. Character Studio used to be an add-on package but is now included with 3ds Max. It has tools to create "smart" skeletons called Bipeds. These skeletons can be animated by using traditional keyframe methods, but they also have the ability to accept motion capture data as well as generate their own walks and runs via footstep-based animation. These animations can be refined by using the traditional tools, but they also can be combined by using the Motion Mixer as well as Motion Flow. Character Studio also includes Physique, a character skinning tool, though any of the 3ds Max skinning tools can be used with Bipeds.

Biped

The heart of Character Studio is the Biped. A **Biped** is a standardized smart skeleton that has joint limits and other information built-in. The Biped can be created from the Systems tab of the Create panel or by choosing Create → Systems → Biped. Left-click and drag in a front viewport to create the Biped.

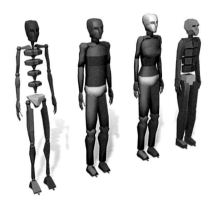

The Biped Create panel allows you to customize the skeleton as it is created. The number of joints in the spine, fingers, toes, and many other parts of the skeleton can be modified.

A basic Biped is a humanlike skeleton. Biped skeletons come in four flavors: Skeleton, Male, Female, and Classic.

Adding leg links (right) creates a dinosaurlike leg structure.

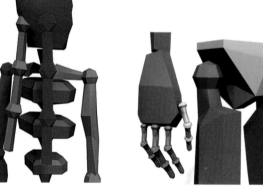

Bipeds can have tails as well as ponytails.

The number of fingers can be adjusted, as well as the number of toes.

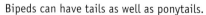
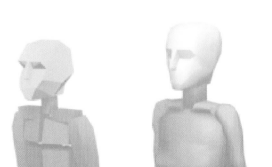

Modifying a Biped

After the Biped is created, modification and animation takes place in the Motion panel. This panel can be used to create, load, and save motions, and to alter the structure of the Biped. The look of the Motion panel changes depending on the selected mode.

Figure mode allows you to refine the structure of the Biped as well as position and scale the Biped's joints. This is the mode used to fit the Biped to a character's mesh. When Figure mode is enabled, the skeleton will snap to the default pose, regardless of any animation applied to the Biped.

Figure Mode Allows the Biped structure to be modified

Footstep Mode Allows footsteps to be created for automatic walks and runs

Biped Playback Plays the Biped animation in wireframe

Selects different parts of the Biped's Center of Mass (COM) object

Motion Flow Mode Allows you to use Biped motions as a script

Mixer Mode Allows you to use Biped motions as motion clips

Save

Load

Allows you to bend and twist multiple joints simultaneously

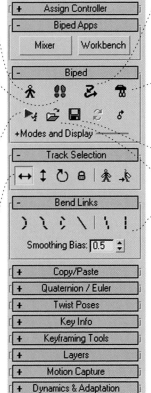

The Biped Motion panel

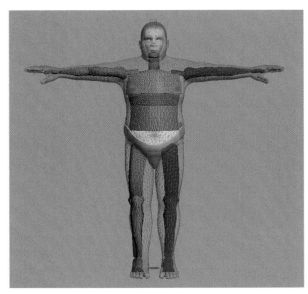

The Biped in Figure mode being fitted to a mesh. Joints can be moved, rotated, or scaled while in Figure mode.

The Figure Mode control panel is very similar to the Create options. The structure of a Biped can be changed here.

Manipulating a Biped

When Figure mode is off, the Biped is ready to be manipulated and animated. A Biped skeleton is a smart skeleton with built-in inverse and forward kinematics. Unlike 3ds Max skeletons, there is no mode that has IK on or off. Rotating any joint in an arm or leg chain initiates forward kinematics, while moving a hand or foot initiates IK. This makes it much easier to pose the character because you don't need to switch modes.

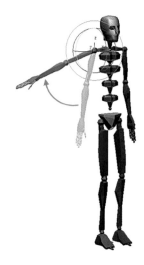

Moving a hand or foot manipulates the joints by using inverse kinematics.

Rotating an arm or leg joint manipulates the joints by using forward kinematics.

The Center of Mass (COM) object is a tetrahedral-shaped object located near the pelvis and is used to move the Biped itself. This differs a bit from other types of skeletons, because normally the pelvis would be used for translation. A Biped, however, does not allow for the pelvis to be moved. Instead, it uses the COM object. The COM takes into account the mass of the Biped, so it is not fixed in relation to the skeleton.

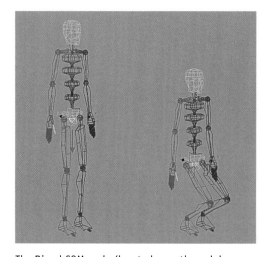

The Biped COM node (located near the pelvis joint) allows you to move and position the body.

Body Horizontal Allows you to move and animate the center of mass horizontally

Body Vertical Allows you to move and animate the center of mass vertically

Body Rotation Allows you to rotate the center of mass

Lock COM Allows you to turn on Body Horizontal, Vertical, and Rotation all at once

Symmetrical Selects symmetrical joints, so selecting the right hand will also select the left

Mirror Selects the same joint (or joints) on the opposite side of the body

The Track Selection rollout gives you tools for manipulating the COM as well as selecting mirror and symmetrical joints on the Biped.

Bend Links mode allows related joints of a Biped to be manipulated all at once. For example, selecting a spine joint with Bend Links activated allows rotation of one spine joint to affect all spine joints.

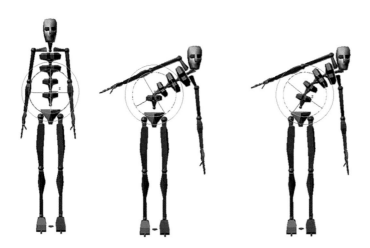

Rotating a spine joint without Bend Links (left). When Bend Links is enabled, all the joints rotate evenly (right).

Keyframing Tools

The Keyframing Tools rollout provides tools to clear and mirror animation on a Biped or selected parts, separate out tracks for keyframing, and anchor joints to a point in space. By default, 3ds Max stores keys for an entire limb rather than the individual joints. Generally, this makes animation easier, because there are fewer tracks. For example, keys for the fingers, hand, forearm, and upper arm are stored in the Clavicle transform track. If you need finer control of the limb, you can use Separate FK Tracks in the Keyframing Tools rollout to add additional control.

Enable Subanims Enables Biped subanims. Subanims allow you to place more than one controller on a Biped joint, such as adding a scale controller to stretch a joint.

Manipulate Subanims Modifies Biped subanims.

Mirror Mirrors the animation and poses on the Biped.

Set Multiple Keys Brings up the Set Multiple Keys dialog box, which allows you to apply incremental changes to a limb.

Creates separate tracks for the selected joints. This lets you keyframe joints separately from the entire limb.

Clear Selected Tracks Clears all keys and constraints from the selected objects and tracks.

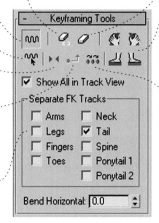

Clear All Animation Clears all keys and constraints from the Biped.

Anchor Limbs Fixes the selected hand or foot to its current position in space. This allows for positioning of the body while keeping the end of the joint stable.

Set Parents Mode When separate FK tracks are used, this will set keys for the parents to the affected joints to store the position of the entire limb. This needs to be on when manipulating a joint by using IK and separate FK tracks.

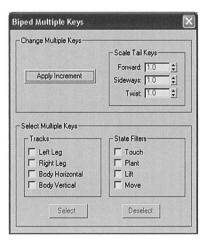

The Biped Multiple Keys dialog box allows you to set multiple keys for a limb. Select the keys in Track view, adjust the limb, and then click Apply Increment.

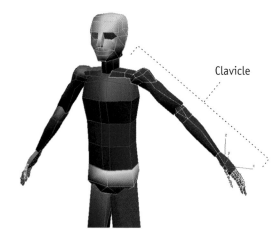

Clavicle

Normally, adjusting any part of a limb sets a key for the entire limb.

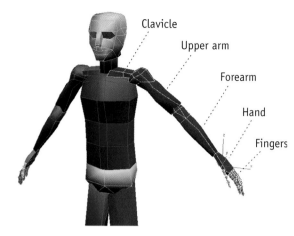

Clavicle

Upper arm

Forearm

Hand

Fingers

Separate FK tracks allow each joint to have its own track.

Anchoring hands or feet allows the body to be positioned and animated while keeping the hands and feet stable.

Key Info

The Key Info rollout allows you to set and modify existing keys as well as view trajectories of Biped joints. Keys can be set for individual joints and limbs as well as for IK. Each type of key has its own rollout that allows you to modify the animation.

Next Key/ Previous Key Jumps between keyframes for the selected Biped joint

Set Key Creates a key at the current frame for selected Biped objects

Delete Key Deletes keys for the selected object at the current frame

Set Planted Key Sets a Biped key with IK set to match the previous IK key, so that the object remains planted

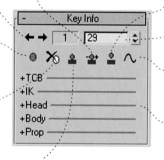

Set Free Key Sets a Biped key with IK off, allowing the object to be animated freely

Set Sliding Key Sets a Biped key with IK not set to match the previous key, so the object is constrained but allowed to slide

Time Indicates the frame number of the current key

Trajectories Shows the trajectories of selected Biped objects

Key Rollouts Allow you to change the keyframe data, depending on the type of object selected

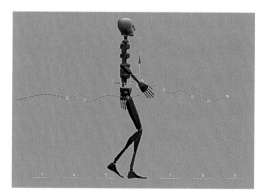

Trajectories show you the motion of a Biped object through the scene.

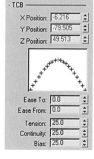

The TCB rollout adjusts keys set with Tension, Continuity, and Bias.

The IK rollout controls limbs that are keyed with IK. When IK Blend is a 1.0, IK is fully active; when it is 0.0, IK is inactive. Join To Prev IK Key sets the position of the current frame to the previous one.

The Body rollout has parameters that apply to the Center of Mass object.

Dynamics

Biped's dynamics use physics to calculate the Biped trajectory when airborne, how the knee bends when landing, and how the Biped maintains balance when the spine is rotated. When the Biped is animated, these parameters adjust the Biped so it adapts to the new position. These parameters are adjusted in the Key Info rollout, under Body. Balance Factor controls where along the spine the Biped's weight is centered. Dynamics Blend controls how gravity affects the Biped when airborne. Ballistic Tension controls how the knee bends to absorb a jump or run step.

The Dynamics & Adaptation rollout allows you to use Biped's dynamics engine and set the value of Gravity. Spline Dynamics turns off the dynamics engine and uses spline-based animation to calculate keyframes.

Animation Workbench

The Animation Workbench is a custom window for manipulating Biped animation curves. It works much the same way as Track view, and has the same Curve Editor, but it also has additional features for working with Biped curves. These tools include analysis functions to check curves for errors and automatically fix them. This is particularly helpful when work-ing with motion capture data, or any animation that is keyframe intensive.

Selects the curves to edit.

Analyzes selected curves.

Fixes analyzed curves.

Filters the curves.

Curves Curves are edited here by using the standard Track View tools.

Controllers Shows the controllers for the selected Biped parts.

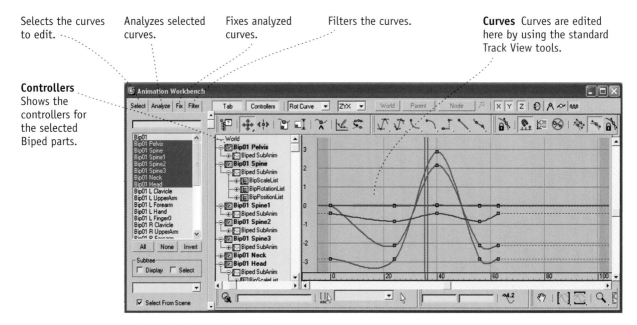

The Animation Workbench window

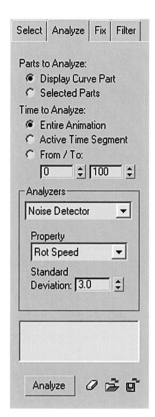

The Analyze tab allows you to analyze selected curves for noise and spikes as well as knee overextension and wobble.

If Analyze produces errors, the Fix tab can automatically correct them. Fixers will adjust the values of keys to smooth out the curve.

Filters can be applied to Biped body parts. They are similar to fixers, but they operate over an interval of time rather than the results of the last analysis. Thus you can use a filter without analyzing.

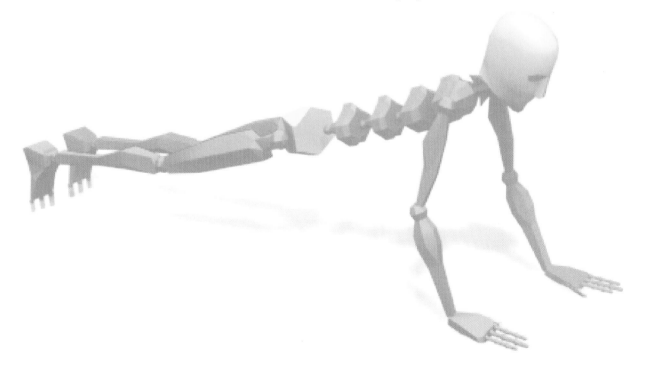

Footstep Animation

Footsteps enable you to take advantage of Biped's built-in dynamics to create simulated human motion. The basic procedure is to lay down footsteps within the scene and then activate them. After this happens, the Biped will automatically walk from footstep to footstep. The walks, runs, and jumps initially created by using footsteps can be somewhat generic, but subsequent keyframe animation can add lots of character to the original animation. Because footsteps are dynamically driven, keyframe animation on certain parts of the character is restricted.

There are two methods of creating footsteps (single or multiple) along with three types of footsteps—walk, run, and jump. The different types of footsteps represent different timings for the footsteps.

Footstep mode Footstep mode can be entered by using either the Sub-Object pull-down or the Footstep icon.

Create Footsteps (Append) Allows you to lay down footsteps interactively. This appends the new footsteps after the last footstep in the animation.

Create Footsteps (At Current Frame) The same as Append, but creates the new footsteps at the current frame. If the new footstep overlaps with an existing footstep, an alert appears.

Create Multiple Footsteps Allows you to create multiple footsteps using user-specified spacing and timing.

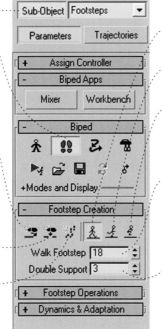

The Biped Motion panel in Footstep mode

Walk Creates new footsteps using walk timing.

Run Creates new footsteps using run timing.

Jump Creates new footsteps using jump timing.

When Walk footsteps are selected, determines the length of a footstep in frames. This spinner changes depending on whether Walk, Run, or Jump is selected.

The amount of time both feet are planted in a walk. This spinner changes depending on whether Walk, Run, or Jump is selected.

Walk: One foot always remains planted while the other swings forward. Walks can also have a portion in the animation called double support, where both feet are on the ground at the same time.

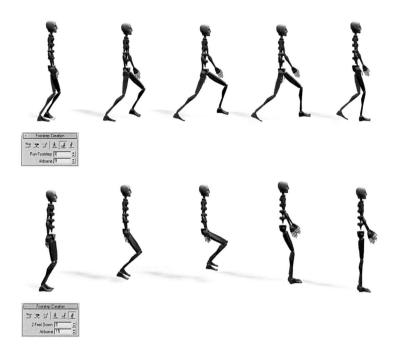

Run: One foot is on the ground at a time with no double support. There is also a point in the animation where both feet are airborne.

Jump: Both feet are on the ground equally or airborne equally.

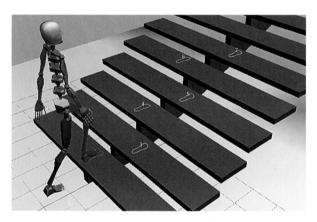

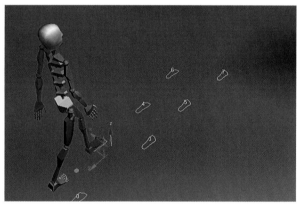

Footsteps can be created one at a time, which can be necessary when a character is walking on an uneven surface, such as these steps.

When the character is walking across a regular surface, Create Multiple Footsteps can be used.

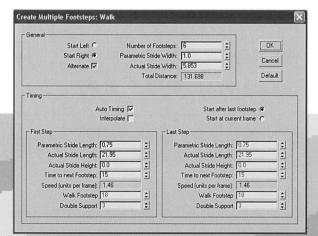

The Create Multiple Footsteps window allows you to define the number of footsteps as well as the lengths and widths of the footsteps.

Activating Footsteps

After footsteps are created, they must be activated. Activation computes the dynamics for the Biped for any footsteps that have been created but not activated. It also creates keys that can be viewed in Track view or the timeline. After footsteps are activated, you can still edit and modify their placement and timing. Footsteps are activated in the Footstep Operations rollout.

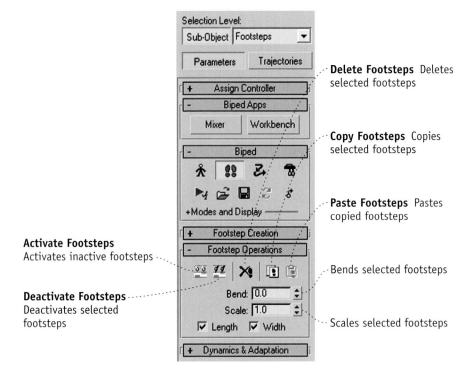

Delete Footsteps Deletes selected footsteps

Copy Footsteps Copies selected footsteps

Paste Footsteps Pastes copied footsteps

Activate Footsteps Activates inactive footsteps

Deactivate Footsteps Deactivates selected footsteps

Bends selected footsteps

Scales selected footsteps

Editing Footsteps

Once activated, footsteps can be edited to change the motion of the Biped. Footsteps can be selected, and then translated or rotated. The Footstep Operations rollout has tools to bend selected footsteps (that is, curve the path of the footsteps) or scale selected footsteps (that is, lengthen or shorten the stride). The timing of the footsteps can be edited in the Dope Sheet.

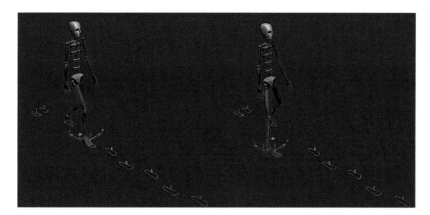

Footsteps can be adjusted and moved after being activated.

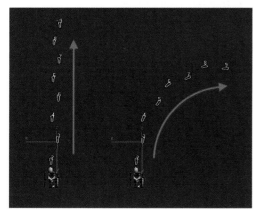

Bend (right) curves the path of the character's walk.

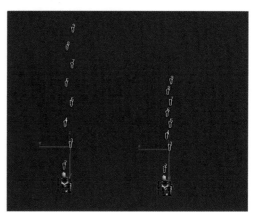

Scale lengthens or shortens the stride length.

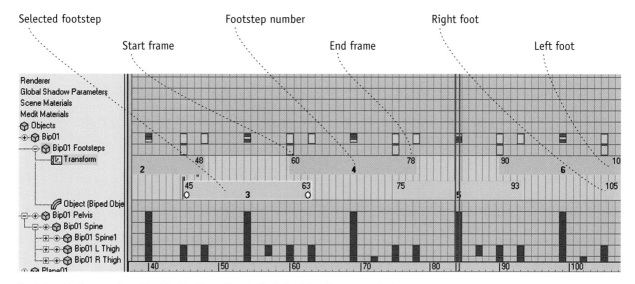

Footstep timing can be edited in the Dope Sheet. Each footstep is represented as a colored block. Blue blocks are left footsteps; green blocks are right footsteps. Clicking a footstep allows you to move it by using the Move Keys tool. Dragging an edge will adjust the length of the footstep.

Using Motion Capture

Motion capture allows you to apply recorded body motion to a Biped. Motion capture systems use markers to record the positions of various body parts over time. This marker data can be applied to a Biped's joints to create motion. Typically, motion capture files record keys at every frame. Biped lets you filter the data as it is applied to the Biped as well as extract footsteps for footstep animation. Motion capture is managed by using the Motion Capture rollout.

Motion capture is imported by using the Load Motion Capture File option in the Motion Capture rollout. 3ds Max supports Biovision (.bvh) and Character Studio (.csm) marker files. When a file is selected, the Motion Capture Conversion Parameters window applies the marker data to parameters that you set.

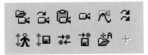

The Motion Capture rollout (above) allows you to load motion capture files and fit the Biped to the talent used for motion capture.

Determines whether footsteps will be extracted from the raw motion capture data. Footsteps can be useful when editing a scene.

Determines whether key reduction will be used.

Sets the tolerances that a foot has to meet to create a footstep.

Determines which frames to load.

Allows for preset files to be used to define the talent's structure.

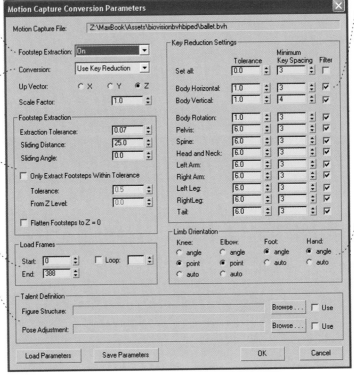

Setting used to reduce keyframes. Filtering determines the minimum space between keys.

Matches the orientation of the Biped limb to the marker file.

Motion Capture Conversion Parameters window

Complex motions, such as dance, work well with motion capture.

After motion capture data is imported into 3ds Max, it can be edited by using the Animation Workbench. Edited motion capture can then be saved in 3ds Max's Biped (.bip) format. A motion that has been converted to Biped format can then be applied to any Biped, regardless of its size and scale.

Motion Flow Mode

Motion Flow uses BIP files as *clips* in a *script*. The motion-flow script joins clips together by using *transitions*. Transitions can be unconditional, chosen at random, or governed by rules such as collision detection. You can control when a transition begins and ends. You can use Motion Flow to animate a single Biped or a crowd of Bipeds.

The Motion Flow rollout allows to to create and save motion scripts.

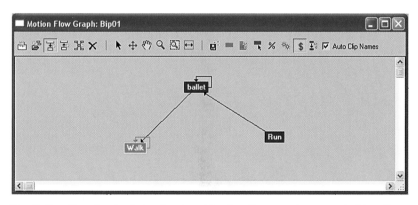

The Motion Flow Graph window is where biped motions can be connected together to create transitions.

Motion Mixer

The Motion Mixer allows you to combine motion clips for both Biped and nonbiped objects. It works very similarly to a nonlinear video editor. Motion is contained in clips, which can contain entire Biped motions or the motions for a single object. Clips are loaded into tracks, which allow you to adjust timing as well as mix transitions from clip to clip. The Motion Mixer lets you to work with animation above the level of the keyframe.

Motion Mixer is used mostly with motion capture files to mix and combine the various takes to create an entire motion. Traditional keyframe animation can also be stored as clips for more-stylized motion. Clips are stored as individual files and are loaded into tracks.

Add Max Objects
Adds objects to the mixer.

Add Bipeds Adds Biped objects to the mixer.

Start frame
The start frame shows at which frame the clip starts.

Weight curve
When weights are animated, a curve shows over the clip. This curve shows how the clip fades in or out.

End frame
Shows the last frame of the clip.

Weighting
Animating this parameter adjusts the weight of the clip, allowing clips to be mixed between tracks.

Track A track can hold multiple clips. Top tracks are processed first.

Active track
The active track is highlighted.

Transition track
When animation needs to be transitioned between two clips, a transition track is used.

Mute Turns off the track.

Solo Turns off all tracks except the solo track.

Transition When two clips in a transition track overlap, a transition appears between them. The edges of the transition can be dragged to adjust its length.

A clip is simply a collection of animation curves. Clips let you gather an object or Biped's keyframe or motion capture data into a single place so you can manipulate the character all at once. Clips are stored on the disk as motion files. They can be Biped (.bip) or Max animation (.xaf) files. Clips are loaded into the Motion Mixer into the selected track or they can also be loaded and stored in the Reservoir.

Clips can be trimmed by selecting an edge of the clip and dragging it.

Transitions have an optimization feature that can automatically find the best timing for a transition between two clips. This is preferable for foot-based animation because you can tell the Motion Mixer to focus on a specific foot.

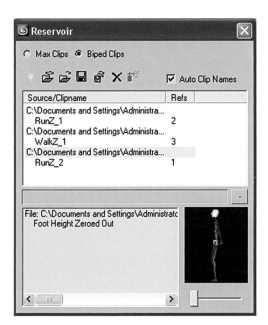

The Reservoir allows you to load clips and manage them.

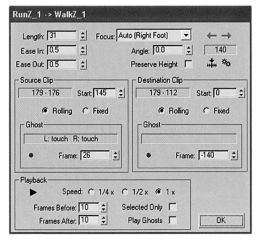

The transition options window

Weighting allows a clip to affect the animation more or less at different times. Weight curves can be adjusted by turning on weighting in the track, and then clicking and dragging the weight curve.

Time Warps allow the animation in a clip to be squashed and stretched over time, allowing a motion to be retimed.

Physique

Physique, similar to the Skin modifier, attaches mesh to a skeleton such as a Biped. When you animate the skeleton with skin attached, Physique deforms the skin to match the skeleton's movement. Physique works on many objects, including geometric primitives, editable meshes, patch-based objects, NURBS, and even FFD space warps. Physique has several advanced features, such as the ability to create bulges, skin sliding, the amount of twist, and crease blending as a character moves. Physique's envelopes are much more customizable than skin, but it does not have Skin's sophisticated vertex weighting or painting and cannot do morph-based deformations.

Applying Physique

Before Physique is applied, the Biped needs to be in Figure mode. As with most characters, it's best to use a pose with the arms outstretched so the hands are away from the torso. This makes initial envelope assignment easier. Apply the Physique modifier to the mesh. The main level of the Physique modifier has a tool called Attach To Node, which attaches the modifier to the root node of the hierarchy. In the case of a Biped, the root node is the Pelvis, not the COM. The COM actually moves as the Biped maintains balance, so that can cause unwanted bulging if it were included in Physique. Once attached, Physique walks the hierarchy and adds all the attached joints. This works differently than Skin because Skin accepts any object as a bone, regardless of hierarchy. To add bones or joints outside of the hierarchy, use Physique's Floating Bones rollout.

Attach To Node Attaches the skin to the root node of a hierarchy.

Reinitialize Resets the action of Physique to defaults.

Level of Detail Options to determine how Physique updates in the viewports and renderer.

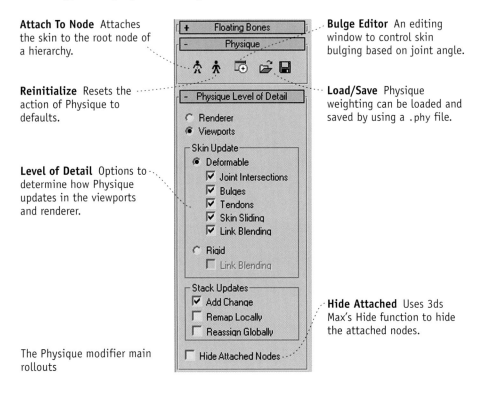

Bulge Editor An editing window to control skin bulging based on joint angle.

Load/Save Physique weighting can be loaded and saved by using a .phy file.

Hide Attached Uses 3ds Max's Hide function to hide the attached nodes.

The Physique modifier main rollouts

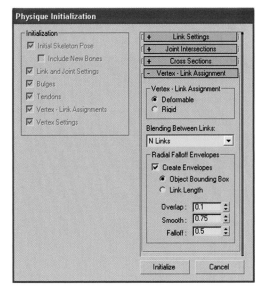

Bones or joints outside of
the hierarchy can be configured by using the Floating
Bones rollout.

When the root node is selected by using Attach To
Node, the initialization window appears.

After Physique has been initialized, adjustment of vertex weights and envelopes can
begin. The process is usually done by adjusting vertices and envelopes first, and then moving on to bulges and tendons. The best way to test how the skin reacts is by animating the
joints of the character so you can adjust Physique parameters and then scrub the timeline
to instantly see the results.

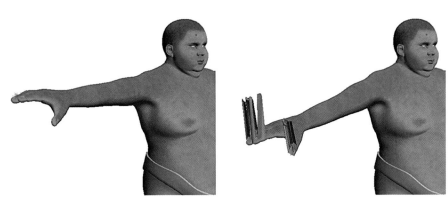

A quick animation of the character will reveal the problem spots. In this case, some of the
finger envelopes need adjusting.

Vertices

The Vertices sub-object determines how each vertex of the mesh will be assigned and how it will deform. Vertices can be assigned to one of three categories: Deformable, Rigid, or Root. Deformable vertices accept deformation from attached nodes and will flex and bend. Rigid vertices move with the attached joint but do not deform. Root vertices do not move with the skeleton.

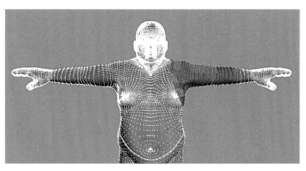

Red vertices deform, such as the vertices in the arm.

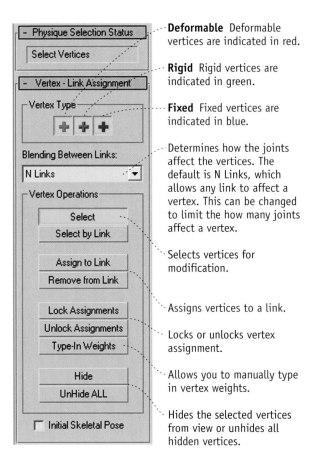

Deformable Deformable vertices are indicated in red.

Rigid Rigid vertices are indicated in green.

Fixed Fixed vertices are indicated in blue.

Determines how the joints affect the vertices. The default is N Links, which allows any link to affect a vertex. This can be changed to limit the how many joints affect a vertex.

Selects vertices for modification.

Assigns vertices to a link.

Locks or unlocks vertex assignment.

Allows you to manually type in vertex weights.

Hides the selected vertices from view or unhides all hidden vertices.

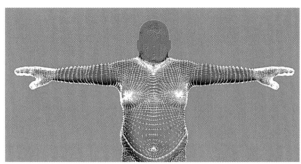

Green vertices move with the joint but remain rigid, such as the head.

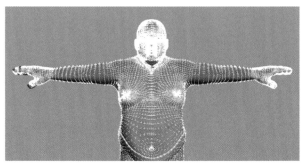

Blue vertices do not move with the mesh. Looking for blue vertices is a good way to chase down unassigned vertices.

Envelopes

Envelopes are the Physique modifier's primary tool for controlling skin deformation. They are accessed by using the Envelopes sub-object. Envelopes work very similarly to the envelopes found in the Skin modifier. Each joint produces a pill-shaped envelope that surrounds the mesh and includes those vertices close to the joint. The size and shape of the envelope can be adjusted. Envelopes can also be set as deformable or rigid. When envelopes overlap, the weighting is balanced between the envelopes. Envelopes have three types of controls: Link, Cross Section, and Control Point. Link is the entire envelope, Cross Section is the radial cross section of the envelope, and Control Points are the points that control the shape of the cross section.

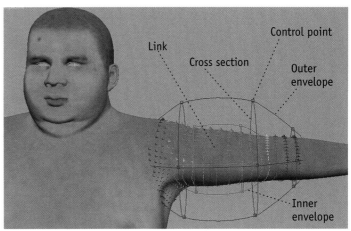

Envelopes surround a joint and include the vertices close to the joint.

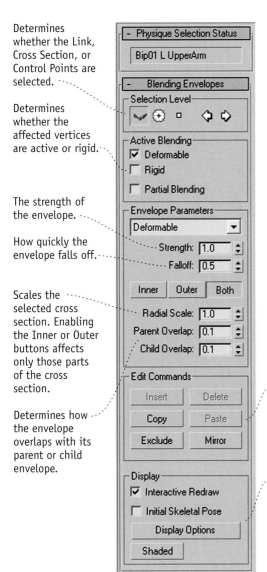

Determines whether the Link, Cross Section, or Control Points are selected.

Determines whether the affected vertices are active or rigid.

The strength of the envelope.

How quickly the envelope falls off.

Scales the selected cross section. Enabling the Inner or Outer buttons affects only those parts of the cross section.

Determines how the envelope overlaps with its parent or child envelope.

Commands to cut and paste envelopes. Mirror is a good way to mirror changes from one side of the character to the other.

Display options for interactivity.

Bulges, Creases, and Other Deformations

In addition to envelopes, Physique has several other methods to deform the mesh based on the movement of the skeleton. Bulges allow the skin to bulge as the joints move. Tendons link one joint to another and spread the effect of moving a joint to the skin around adjacent joints. Link Settings determine how the skin between joints behaves, such as the crease of an elbow.

Bulges can be accessed by using the Bulge sub-object, but there is also a floating Bulge Editor window that provides a graphical interface. Bulging is configured by animating the joint and setting bulge angles for each point. For the bulging of a bicep, for example, the elbow would be animated straight and at 90 degrees to create two bulge angles. Then using the Bulge Editor or the interactive tools in the viewport, the cross sections and control points are reshaped to create the desired bulge at each angle.

Similar to envelopes, each bulge has joints, cross sections, and control points.

These buttons set, insert, and delete bulge angles from the pull-down list.

The range of angles through which the bulge influences the skin.

Controls how smoothly or abruptly the bulge takes effect.

Increases the effect of the current bulge angle relative to the effect of any other bulges.

Tools to configure and modify cross sections.

The selected bulge angle as configured in the Bulge Angle Parameters section. The bulge angle can be changed by pulling down the list.

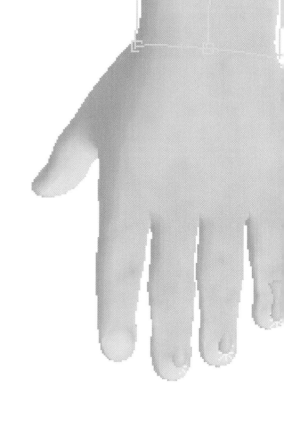

The Bulge sub-object rollout

This bicep bulges as the elbow moves. Notice how the cross sections surrounding the arm change shape.

Control Point tools Tools to draw, create, and delete control points.

Cross Section tools Tools to create, delete, and adjust cross sections.

Bulge Angle tools These buttons set, insert, and delete bulge angles from the pull-down list.

Bulge angle The selected bulge angle. The bulge angle can be changed by pulling down the list.

Bulge angle parameters Influence, Power, and Weight parameters, exactly the same as in the Bulge sub-object rollout.

Select and Translate Tools to select, move, rotate, and scale control points.

Bulge profile The profile of the bulge is displayed graphically.

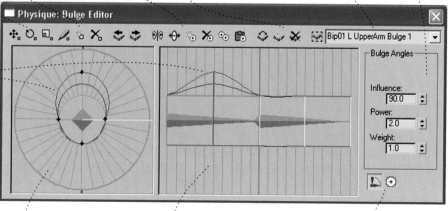

Radial view

Side view

Cross Section/Bulge Angle Switches between Cross Section and Bulge Angle mode.

The Bulge Editor allows you to graphically edit skin bulging.

Affects the pivot point where vertices are bent. Normally this is the pivot point of the joint, but this can be changed if joint placement is off.

Controls the way the skin deforms when a joint rotates along its length, such as when the wrist turns.

Skin sliding controls how the skin slides when a joint rotates. Without skin sliding, vertices closest to the joint tend to compress on the inside and pull apart on the outside.

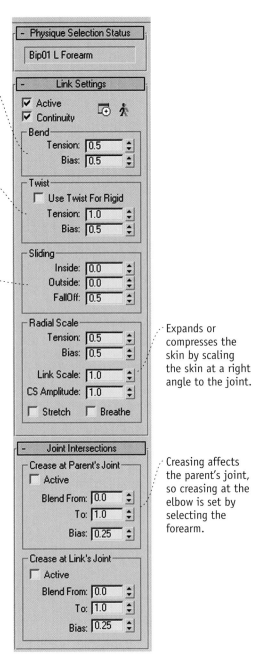

Expands or compresses the skin by scaling the skin at a right angle to the joint.

Creasing affects the parent's joint, so creasing at the elbow is set by selecting the forearm.

The Link Settings sub-object rollout contains options to affect how skin slides, twists, and creases.

The Tendons sub-object roll-out controls the behavior of tendons, which spread the effect of moving a joint to the skin around adjacent joints.

Animating a Biped

1 Load the file Biped_Start.max. It contains a Biped and some stairs. We're going to make the Biped walk up the stairs and jump off.

2 Select the Biped and activate the Motion panel. Enable Footstep mode.

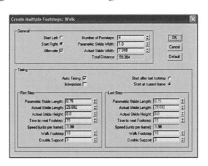

3 Select the Create Multiple Footsteps option. A window appears. Use the defaults to create four footsteps.

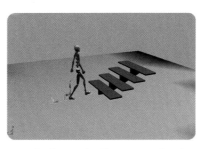

4 Activate the footsteps. Scrub the animation to see the Biped walk.

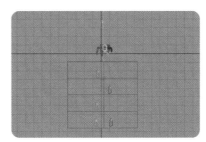

5 Now we need to walk the Biped up the stairs. Select the Create Footsteps (Append) option. From the top viewport, create one footstep for each stairstep starting with the right foot. At the top stairstep, create two footsteps.

6 Drawing the footsteps in the top viewport places them at ground level. Use the Move tool to position the footsteps on the stairsteps.

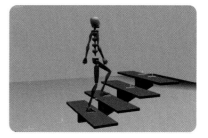

7 Activate the new footsteps. Scrub the animation to see the Biped walk up the stairs.

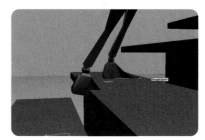

8 There may be places in the animation where the Biped's foot passes through the stairs.

9 If this is the case, exit Footstep mode and turn on Auto Key. Scrub the point where the foot hits the stairs and animate the foot out of the way.

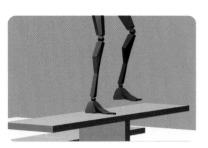

10 At the end of the animation, the Left foot lifts up. We need to fix this so that the character can leap from both feet planted.

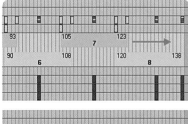

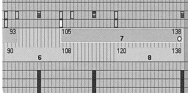

11 Open the Dope Sheet and expand the Bip01 Footsteps track. At the end of the animation, you'll see that the left foot (blue) rises off the ground at frame 123, while the right foot (green) stays planted to frame 138. Grab the edge of the left footstep and drag it to 138.

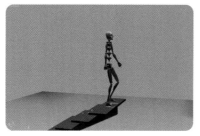

12 This corrects the foot placement but still leaves animation. We need to delete this and keyframe the Biped manually in preparation for the jump.

13 Double-click the Biped pelvis and delete the keys at frames 131 and 138.

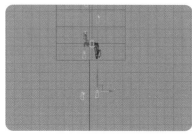

14 Select the Create Footsteps (At Current Frame) option. Scrub to frame 150. Set the type of footstep to Jump and lay down two footsteps on the floor in front of the last stairstep.

15 Activate the footsteps and scrub the time slider to see the character jump. The motion is rather generic, but you can add more life to it by using traditional keyframe techniques.

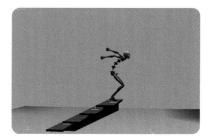

16 Turn off Footstep mode and scrub the animation back to frame 138 (where the leap starts). Turn on Auto Key and create a pose with the arms back and the body bent forward.

17 Scroll to frame 144 and create a pose with the arms forward and the knees bent.

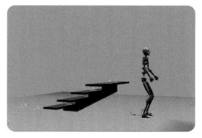

18 Continue to modify the animation to suit your tastes.

Special Effects

3 ds Max is used as a special effects tool in the film, video, and game industries. Special effects can be created in various ways, but many of the best special effects simulate reality. 3ds Max has tools for creating and animating objects that respond to real-world forces such as gravity. Objects animated in this way can appear highly realistic and can seamlessly blend with real-world scenes.

Particles simulate the motion of large numbers of objects and are terrific for all sorts of fire, water, and atmospheric effects. 3ds Max has several basic types of particle systems, as well as Particle Flow, which offers much more sophisticated tools.

Reactor's dynamics allow objects to animate and collide with each other by using forces, and soft body dynamics allow physical forces to affect the actual shape of an object.

Particle Systems

Particle systems are used to simulate all sorts of natural phenomena, from smoke and fire to rain, sparks, and any other effect that requires animating a large number of objects. In 3ds Max, there are several types of particle systems. Basic particle systems allow for simple simulations such as a spray or cloud of particles. These basic systems can be affected by forces so they can interact with an environment. For more-sophisticated applications, Particle Flow is an event-driven system that allows for a high degree of control over particle behavior.

Basic Particle Systems

3ds Max has several types of basic particle systems, also called nonevent particle systems. These provide straightforward tools for creating simple effects such as snow, rain, exhaust, water sprays, and more. These particle systems are located in the Create tab.

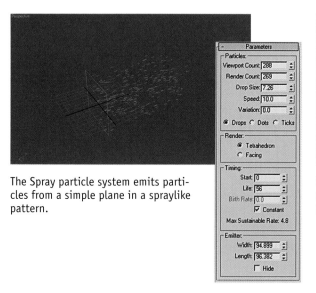

The Spray particle system emits particles from a simple plane in a spraylike pattern.

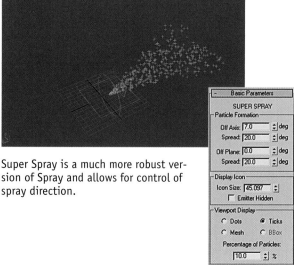

Super Spray is a much more robust version of Spray and allows for control of spray direction.

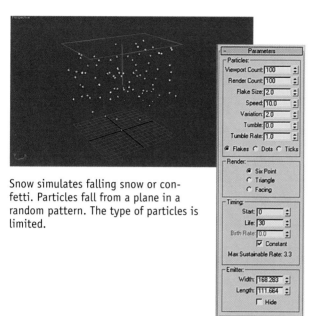

Snow simulates falling snow or con-fetti. Particles fall from a plane in a random pattern. The type of particles is limited.

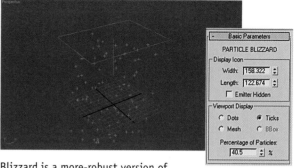

Blizzard is a more-robust version of snow and can create more types of par-ticles, including metaparticles and instanced geometry.

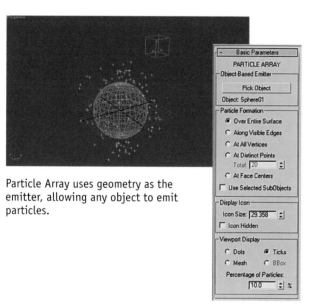

Particle Array uses geometry as the emitter, allowing any object to emit particles.

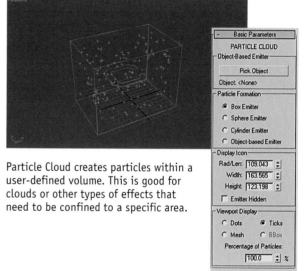

Particle Cloud creates particles within a user-defined volume. This is good for clouds or other types of effects that need to be confined to a specific area.

Particle Types

Each particle system is slightly different, but they can create many of the same types of particles. These can be standard particles, instanced geometry, or blobby metaparticles.

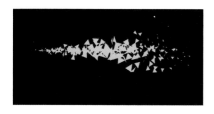

Triangle creates flat triangular shaped particles.

Special creates particle shapes consisting of three intersecting planes.

Constant creates circular-shaped particles.

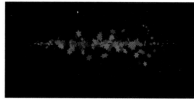

SixPoint creates particles shaped like six-pointed stars.

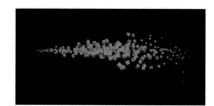

Cube creates cube-shaped particles.

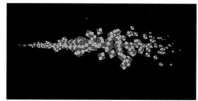

Facing creates planar particles that always face the camera.

Tetra creates tetrahedral-shaped particles.

Sphere creates spherical particles.

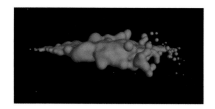

Metaparticles are blobby particles that create fluidlike effects.

Instanced Geometry allows you to use any 3ds Max object as a particle.

The Particle Type rollout, available in Super Spray, Blizzard, PArray, and PCloud, contains all the basic particle types.

Particle Generation

In addition to the type of particle, the particle system needs to know how the particles will be generated. This information includes the number of particles, their speed, and the length of time that the particles will live.

Use Rate creates a specific number of particles per frame. Use Total creates a fixed number of particles over the life of the system.

Determines the speed of the particles with a Variation control to randomize the speed.

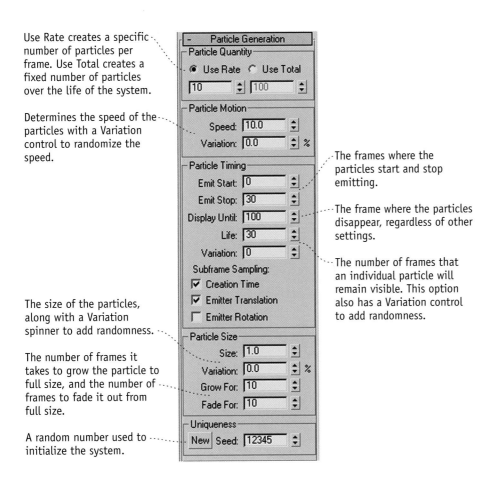

The frames where the particles start and stop emitting.

The frame where the particles disappear, regardless of other settings.

The number of frames that an individual particle will remain visible. This option also has a Variation control to add randomness.

The size of the particles, along with a Variation spinner to add randomness.

The number of frames it takes to grow the particle to full size, and the number of frames to fade it out from full size.

A random number used to initialize the system.

Particle Motion

In addition to speed, particles can rotate and collide with each other as well as spawn
new particles when they collide with other objects. This adds another layer of realism to
the system.

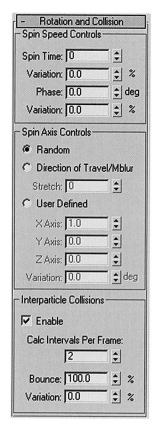

Rotation And Collision
defines how particles spin
as well as how they behave
when they collide with each
other.

Object Motion Inheritance
determines how particles will
be affected by the movement
of the emitter.

Bubble Motion simulates the
wobble effect that happens
in bubbles rising underwater.
Typically, it's used when the
particles are set to rise in
thin streams.

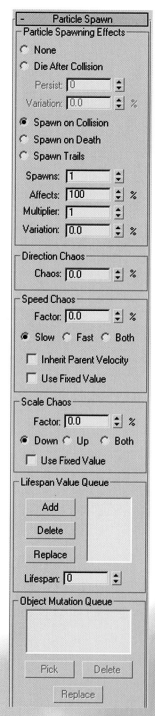

Particle Spawn
allows new
particles to be
created when they
collide or die.

Texturing Particles

Particles can be textured by using the standard 3ds Max materials. This is good for pure color, but when particles need to have texture applied, face mapping must be used. This can be set in the Material Editor.

This bitmap is used in the Diffuse channel of a material.

When it is applied to this particle system, the mapping is calculated over the entire particle system.

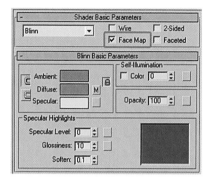

Selecting the Face Map check box inside the material resolves the problem.

The bitmap is now mapped to each individual particle.

Many types of effects require that the particles change color over the course of their lifetimes. A red fire particle, for example, might change into a gray particle as it ages to simulate fire turning into smoke. Some effects can require a particle's opacity to change as it gets older. This can be done by using the Particle Age mapping type.

The color of the map.

Map Instead of color, maps can also be used.

The point in the particle's life that the color is reached.

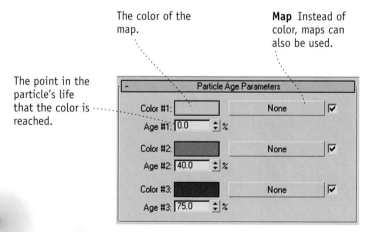

The Particle Age map changes the color of the map throughout the particle's life.

In this case, the exhaust goes from orange to red to dark gray.

Forces

The motion of particles can be affected by forces. **Forces** can create such effects as gravity, wind, and vortex. Forces are found in the Create panel, under Space Warps. To connect a particle system to a force, select the particle system, press the Bind To Space Warp icon, and drag the line to the force icon.

Gravity pulls particles in a specific direction, usually toward the ground.

Wind is similar to gravity but can have turbulence.

Vortex creates a radial vortex. Vortex is useful for creating black holes, whirlpools, tornadoes, and other funnel-like objects.

Path Follow allows particles to follow a spline path, in this case, a star.

Motor applies a rotational force to a particle system.

Deflectors

Deflectors allow particles to collide with objects. Deflectors are found on the Space Warps tab of the Create panel. Deflectors can take the shape of planes or spheres and can also use 3ds Max geometry as the deflector objects.

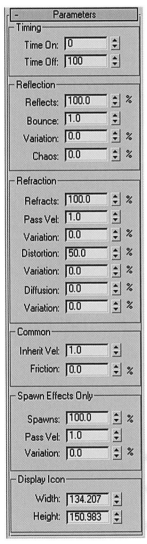

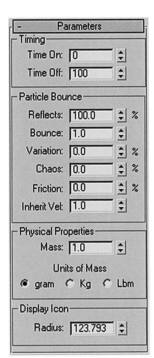

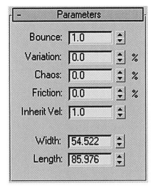

The standard deflectors are Deflector, which is a planar-shaped deflector, SDeflector, which is spherical, and UDeflector, which uses geometry.

Deflectors allow particles to collide and to be deflected by objects.

DynaFlect deflectors allow the force of a particle system to affect actual objects in a 3ds Max scene. This allows a fire hose to knock over an object, for example.

OmniFlect deflectors come in three types: POmniFlect is planar shaped, SOmniFlect is spherical, and UOmniFlect uses geometry. OmniFlect deflectors have additional parameters for chaos, reflection, and refraction.

Particle Flow

Particle Flow is an event-driven particle system. Creation of a Particle Flow system starts with creating a PF Source particle system. Once created, Particle Flow systems can be built and modified in the Particle View window. Within this window, you can add events and operators to the system that can affect almost any aspect of the particles.

Global Event This is the first event in the system and has the same name as the PF Source icon in the scene.

Event Display This window contains all the events.

Help Highlighting an object in the depot displays help about its purpose here.

Parameters Shows the parameters for the highlighted part of the event window.

Link Links connect two events together.

Events These affect the behavior of the particle system.

Depot The depot contains operators that can be dragged into the Event Display, where they can be wired into the system.

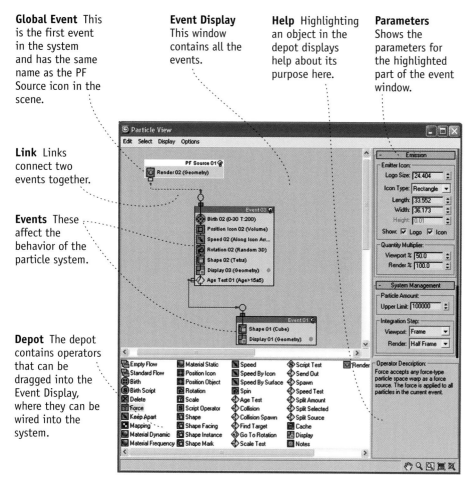

Particle View is the main interface for Particle Flow.

Particle Flow starts by creating a PF Source particle system.

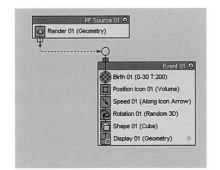

This particle system has cubes being emitted toward the hemisphere.

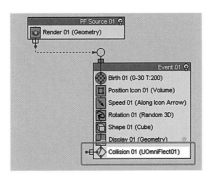

A collision is added, and the sphere is set as the collision object by using UDeflector. This causes the cubes to be deflected by the hemisphere.

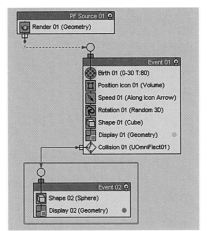

A new event is added, and the Shape parameter is set to create spheres. This event is wired to the collision to change the cubes into spheres as they deflect.

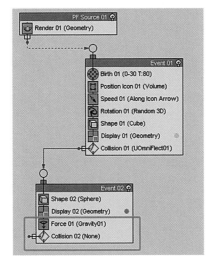

A force is added and con-nected to gravity. A collision is also added to the event to make the sphere particles bounce off the hemisphere as they fall.

Reactor

Reactor animates objects automatically to simulate the effect of real-world forces and collisions. Reactor can create rigid bodies, which do not deform as they collide, or soft bodies, which change shape as they collide and move. Reactor creates highly realistic looking animation and is good for simulating natural motion.

Reactor has its own menu on the main menu bar, which contains all of reactor's objects and modifiers, as well as tools to define object properties and to create and preview animations. Reactor objects can also be found in the Create panel, under Helpers. The Utilities panel also has a Reactor button that allows you to configure the dynamics engine and create animations.

Rigid Body Dynamics

Reactor can create rigid body dynamics to simulate how physical objects move in the real world. These tools can be used to simulate objects falling, colliding, or being affected by physical forces such as wind and gravity. The solutions can be physically accurate, making the result very realistic.

Creating a Simulation

Rigid body simulations are set up by creating a rigid body collection containing each object in the simulation, defining each object's physical properties, adding in forces, and then running the simulation.

A basic scene with a ball bouncing down stairs and knocking over some boxes

Create a rigid body collection (reactor → Create Object → Rigid Body Collection). This is a list containing all the objects in the simulation. Objects can be picked individually from a viewport or added from the list.

After the properties are set up, the animation can be created. The reactor tab of the Utilities panel contains tools to create and preview the animation.

Each object has a set of object properties that define physical properties about the object such as mass, friction, and elasticity. These are accessed via reactor → Open Property Editor. Objects that remain passive, such as the walls and the floor, are given a mass of zero, while active objects, such as the ball and boxes, are given masses larger than zero.

The tab also contains a rollout for configuring the parameters of the world, such as the force of gravity.

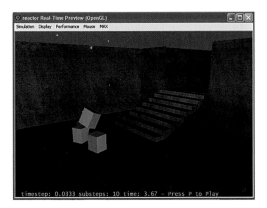

Animation previews appear in the Real-Time Preview window

When the preview is approved, the final animation can be generated. This creates keyframes for all the objects in the scene.

Forces

In addition to reactor's built-in gravity, other forces can be used to create more-realistic animations.

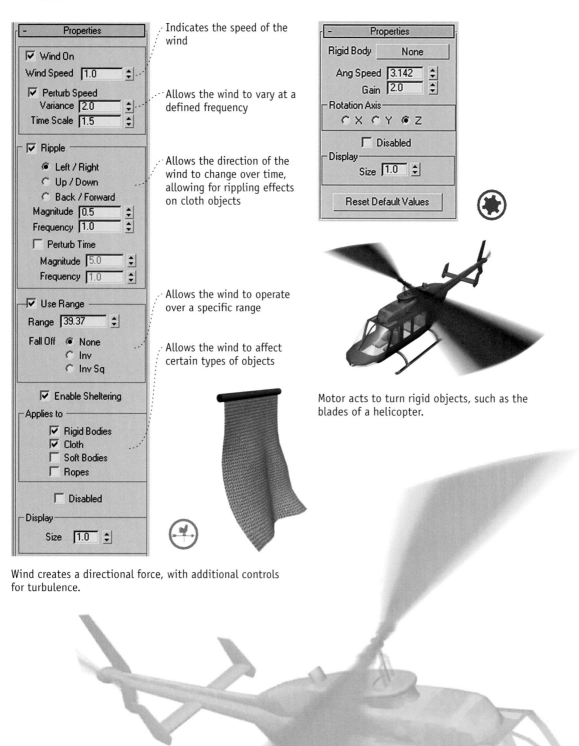

Indicates the speed of the wind

Allows the wind to vary at a defined frequency

Allows the direction of the wind to change over time, allowing for rippling effects on cloth objects

Allows the wind to operate over a specific range

Allows the wind to affect certain types of objects

Wind creates a directional force, with additional controls for turbulence.

Motor acts to turn rigid objects, such as the blades of a helicopter.

Constraints

Constraints let you restrict how objects move in the simulation. They can fix objects to each other or let them move only in specific ways.

The Hinge constraint allows you to simulate a hingelike action between two bodies.

The Point-Point (point-to-point) constraint lets you attach two objects together. The objects can rotate in relation to each other, but always have the attachment point in common.

The Point-Path constraint allows you to constrain two bodies so that the child can move along a path relative to the parent, much like a bead on a wire.

The Prismatic constraint allows its bodies to move relative to each other along one axis only.

You can use the Carwheel constraint to attach a wheel to another object—for instance, a car chassis. You can also constrain a wheel to a position in world space. During the simulation, the wheel object is free to rotate around a spin axis defined in each object's space.

The Ragdoll constraint lets you realistically simulate the behavior of body joints, such as hips, shoulders, and ankles. This is very useful for creating digital stuntmen.

The Spring constraint lets you create a springlike effect between two rigid bodies in the simulation, or between a rigid body and a point in space.

Helpers

Helpers let you define specific types of simulations, such as an automobile or a fracturing object.

Fracture simulates the breaking of a rigid body into pieces as the result of an impact. To do this, you need to create the pieces that are glued together to create the whole object.

Toy Car simulates a simple car without having to set up each constraint separately. This option lets you choose a chassis and wheels for your car, tweak various properties such as the strength of its suspension, and specify whether you would like reactor to turn its wheels during the simulation.

Soft Bodies

Soft bodies are objects that change shape when affected by forces and motion. They are great for secondary motion such as a waving flag, a jiggling belly, or a dog's floppy ears. Soft bodies are similar to cloth, the main difference between them being that soft bodies have a sense of shape. A soft body will tend to return to its original shape after motion settles.

Soft bodies are created by using a soft body collection and a soft body modifier. The modifier is applied to a mesh to add soft body properties, and these are then collected for simulation. Soft body simulation is done by using the same tools as for rigid body simulations, and soft bodies can interact with rigid bodies.

 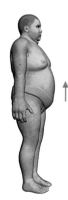 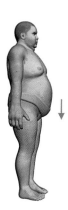

Soft bodies can be used to make this character's belly jiggle.

The mass of the object.

The stiffness of the soft body. Lower values make the object easier to deform.

Damps oscillations through the soft body.

Coefficient of friction for the surface of the soft body.

The default, used when the modifier is applied to a mesh.

Used when the modifier is applied to an FFD.

Allows you to exclude vertices from the soft body simulation or attach them to other objects.

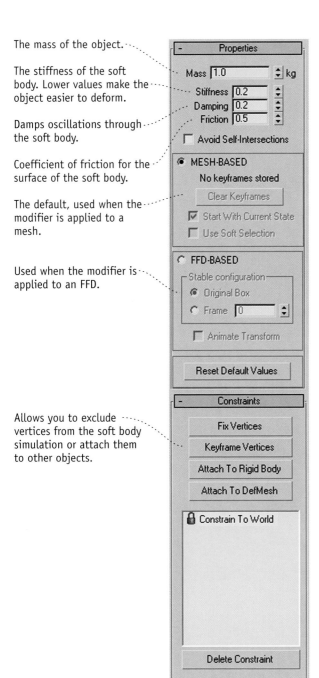

The soft body modifier (reactor → Apply Modifier → Soft Body Modifier) allows an object to behave as a soft body.

The soft body collection (reactor → Create Object → Soft Body Collection) incorporates all of the objects with soft body modifiers into the simulation.

Soft bodies can also be used to deform FFDs, which in turn deform meshes. This can help speed processing with complex meshes.

Cloth

Cloth in reactor creates simple cloth objects, such as curtains, flags, or capes. More-complex garments can be created by using 3ds Max's cloth system. Cloth works much in the same way as soft bodies, but unlike soft bodies, cloth does not retain the original shape of the object.

Cloth is created by using a cloth collection and a cloth modifier. The modifier is applied to a mesh to add soft body properties, and these are then collected for simulation. Soft body simulation is done by using the same tools as for rigid body simulations, and soft bodies can interact with rigid bodies.

Cloth can interact with rigid body simulations.

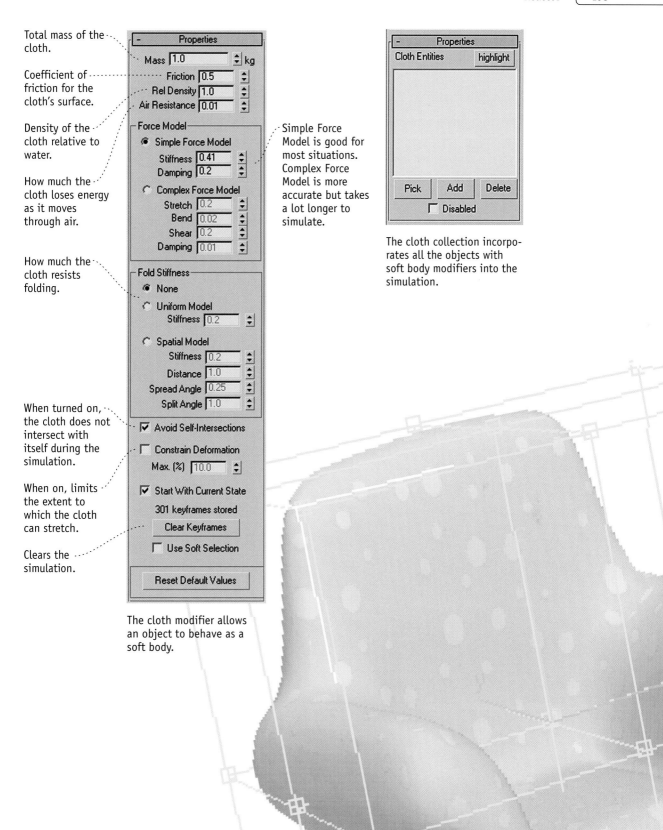

Total mass of the cloth.

Coefficient of friction for the cloth's surface.

Density of the cloth relative to water.

How much the cloth loses energy as it moves through air.

How much the cloth resists folding.

When turned on, the cloth does not intersect with itself during the simulation.

When on, limits the extent to which the cloth can stretch.

Clears the simulation.

Simple Force Model is good for most situations. Complex Force Model is more accurate but takes a lot longer to simulate.

The cloth collection incorporates all the objects with soft body modifiers into the simulation.

The cloth modifier allows an object to behave as a soft body.

Simulating Collisions

1 Open the file `Reactor_Start.max`. This has a simple room with some stairs.

2 Create a sphere.

3 Open the Object Properties window (reactor → Open Property Editor). Set the mass of the ball to 100.

4 Create a box in the scene. As with the sphere, open the Object Properties window (reactor → Open Property Editor). Set the mass of the box to 15.

5 Duplicate the box several times and create a stack of boxes to knock over. Make sure the boxes are not overlapping with each other or the floor.

6 Create a rigid body collection (reactor → Create Object → Rigid Body Collection) in the scene.

7 In the rigid body collection Modify panel, add all the geometry in the scene.

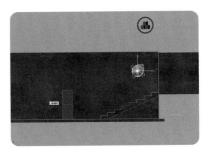

8 Position the sphere above the stairs.

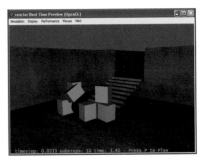

9 Run a preview (reactor → Preview Animation) to see how the animation works. If you want to make changes, simply move the objects in the scene around and make another preview.

10 When you're satisfied with the preview, create the animation (reactor → Create Animation). This will generate keyframes for all the objects in the scene. Render your final scene.

Hair and Cloth

3 ds Max has some very sophisticated tools to create hair and cloth. Creating realistic hair and cloth has always been a difficult task for 3D animators. The complex calculations required to create these surfaces make it a computing-intensive task.

Hair and Fur

Getting hair to perform properly requires software that allows you to create, style, color, and add dynamics to the hair. 3ds Max uses hair technology originally created for Joe Alter's Shave and a Haircut software, which is available for most major 3D packages. Hair can be used for creating creatures, but it can also be used for other natural effects, such as grass, foliage, and feathers. Hair is applied as a modifier, but renders separately from the objects in a 3ds Max scene and is composited back into the image as a render effect.

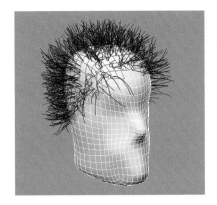

Hair can be applied to an entire object or to part of an object by using sub-object selections.

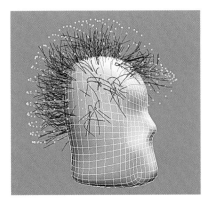

Guide sub-objects are hairs used to direct the general flow of the hair. They can be displayed separately or with the other hair by using the Display rollout.

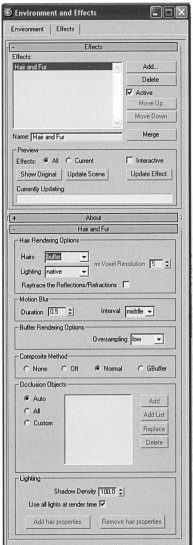

Hair is rendered as a render effect, with the hair composited into the scene after rendering is complete.

Creating Hair and Fur

Hair is created by applying the Hair And Fur modifier (Modifiers → Hair And Fur → Hair And Fur (WSM) to any type of geometry. The Hair modifier has several rollouts used to create the overall look of the hair. These control the overall length and distribution of the hair as well as the hair color. Additional parameters such as kinkiness and frizziness can also be configured.

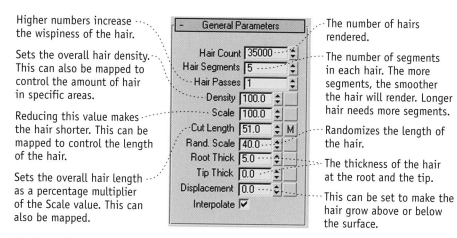

Higher numbers increase the wispiness of the hair.

Sets the overall hair density. This can also be mapped to control the amount of hair in specific areas.

Reducing this value makes the hair shorter. This can be mapped to control the length of the hair.

Sets the overall hair length as a percentage multiplier of the Scale value. This can also be mapped.

The number of hairs rendered.

The number of segments in each hair. The more segments, the smoother the hair will render. Longer hair needs more segments.

Randomizes the length of the hair.

The thickness of the hair at the root and the tip.

This can be set to make the hair grow above or below the surface.

The General Parameters rollout creates the basic length and thickness of the hair.

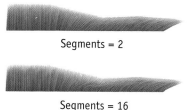

Segments = 2

Segments = 16

More hair segments allow the hair to flow more smoothly.

Parameters such as length and density can be mapped to control distribution of the hair.

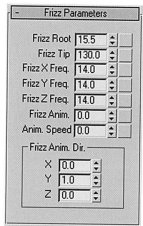

The Frizz Parameters rollout is similar to the Kink Parameters rollout but allows for animation. This can be useful for short hairstyles that may not need dynamics.

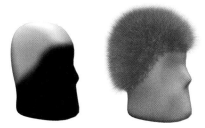

The distribution of the hair on this head is controlled by using a map. In this case, the white areas of the bitmap control the distribution.

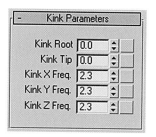

The Kink Parameters rollout allows you to create waves or kinks in the hair. The parameters allow for a wave frequency to be applied as well as to affect the root or the tip more.

Texturing Hair

The Material Parameters rollout has parameters that define the color of the hair. Hair color can change from root to tip, and mutant hairs can add random color. Most parameters can be mapped to create patterns.

When rendered in mental ray, will fade the hair to transparent at its tip.

The color of the tip of the hair.

The color of the hair at the root.

The brightness of the highlights on the hair.

The size of the specular highlights.

Shadowing Allows the hair to cast shadows, self-shadow, and receive shadows from other geometry.

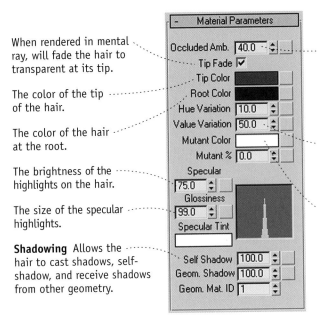

Controls the contrast of the hair rendering by affecting the Ambient and Diffuse channels. Higher values render the hair with less contrast.

Parameters to vary the hair color by varying the hue and value of the root and tip colors.

Introduces mutant hairs of the defined color. The Mutant % spinner controls the percentage of mutant hairs.

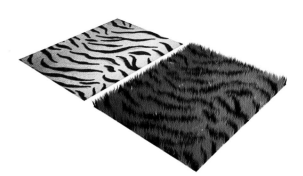

Many of the material parameters can be mapped, such as color.

Mutant Color mixes in random hairs of a specified color.

Styling Hair

Hair can be styled by using tools that are similar to those of a hair stylist. These include brushes, combs, and clippers. Styling tools aren't available until you click Style Hair to turn on styling, or choose the Guides sub-object level in either the Selection rollout or the modifier stack. The styling tools affect these guides, which in turn affect the rendered hairs.

Selecting Guides

The complete hairstyle can be styled by using the styling tools, but for better control, you can select guides individually before styling to affect specific areas of the hair. Guides are selected by using the tools in the Selection section of the dialog box. The entire guide or individual parts, such as the end, root, or individual vertices, can be selected by using the standard 3ds Max selection tools.

Style Hair/Finish Styling This button activates the styling tools. It is the same as selecting the Guides sub-object.

Selection Allows you to select by end, guides, vertices, or root.

Marker Type Pull-down that determines how markers are displayed: Box, Plus, X, or Dot.

Invert Inverts the selection.

Rotate Rotates the selection.

Expand Expands the selection.

Hide/Show Hides the current selection or shows all hidden selections.

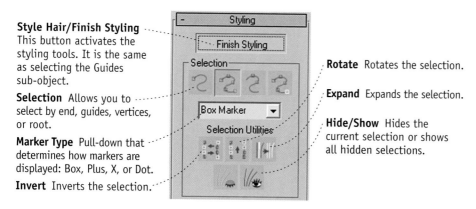

The selection tools select guides or parts of guides for styling.

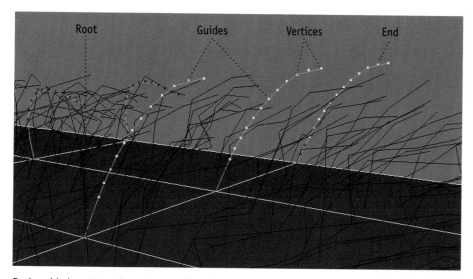

Each guide has 14 vertices that can be selected individually to affect only parts of the guide.

Styling Tools

The styling tools allow you to select, brush, and cut the hair. When Selection is active, individual guides can be selected by using the selection tools. The Hair Brush tool allows you to move hair; the Hair Cut tool shortens the hair.

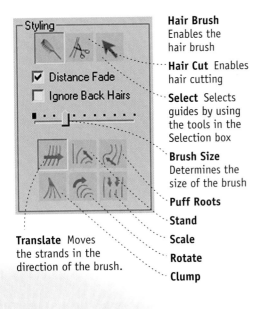

Hair Brush Enables the hair brush

Hair Cut Enables hair cutting

Select Selects guides by using the tools in the Selection box

Brush Size Determines the size of the brush

Puff Roots

Stand

Scale

Rotate

Clump

Translate Moves the strands in the direction of the brush.

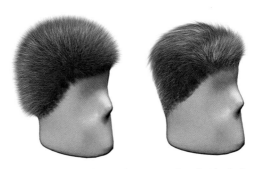

Styling tools can be used to cut and style the hair.

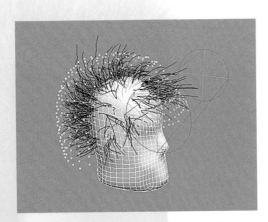

Hair Brush Dragging the brush (green) affects the selected guides. The action of the brush depends on the selected tool, such as Translate, Stand, Puff Roots, and so forth.

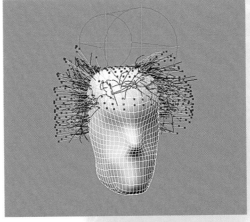

Hair Cut Lets you trim the guide hairs. This doesn't actually remove vertices; it only scales the guide hairs. You can restore guide hairs to their original length with Scale or one of the Pop commands found in the Utilities panel.

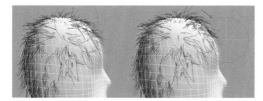

Puff Roots Similar to Stand, but weights the effect toward the roots of the hair.

Stand Stands the hairs up by making them perpendicular to the surface.

Clump Forces selected guides to move toward each other (left-mouse drag) or farther apart (right-mouse drag).

Rotate Rotates the guides, creating a tangled hair effect.

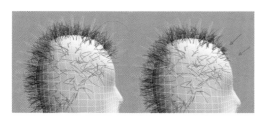

Scale Scales selected guides larger (right-mouse drag) or smaller (left-mouse drag).

Translate Moves selected guides in the direction that you drag the mouse.

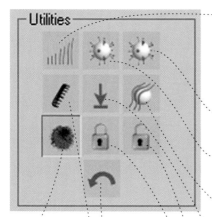

Attenuate Length Scales selected guides according to the surface. This can be useful in applying fur to an animal model, which typically has smaller polygons in areas with shorter hair.

Pop Zero-Sized Like Pop Selected, but works on zero-length hairs.

Pop Selected Pops selected hairs out along the surface normal.

Toggle Collisions Takes the collisions between hair strands into account when styling.

Reset Rest Averages hair guides by using the growth mesh's connectivity. Particularly useful after using Recomb.

Lock/Unlock Locks and unlocks selected guides.

Toggle Hair Toggles view-port display of generated hair but doesn't affect display of the hair guides.

Undo Undoes the last hair operation.

Recomb Flattens the hair by placing the guides parallel to the surface.

The Recomb tool flattens the hair.

The Utilities section contains various tools to work with hair.

Dynamics

For hair to seem natural in an animation, it must move naturally when the body moves and also respond to such forces as wind and gravity. Hair's Dynamics rollout contains tools to let the hair behave like real-world hair. Hair dynamics can be viewed interactively in the viewport by using Live mode, or you can choose Precomputed mode for rendering.

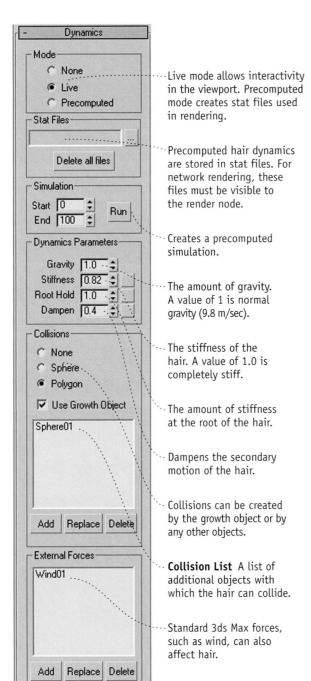

Live mode allows interactivity in the viewport. Precomputed mode creates stat files used in rendering.

Precomputed hair dynamics are stored in stat files. For network rendering, these files must be visible to the render node.

Creates a precomputed simulation.

The amount of gravity. A value of 1 is normal gravity (9.8 m/sec).

The stiffness of the hair. A value of 1.0 is completely stiff.

The amount of stiffness at the root of the hair.

Dampens the secondary motion of the hair.

Collisions can be created by the growth object or by any other objects.

Collision List A list of additional objects with which the hair can collide.

Standard 3ds Max forces, such as wind, can also affect hair.

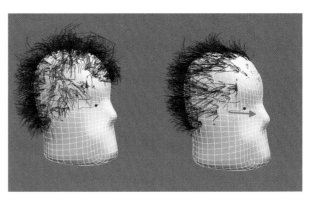

When Live mode is enabled, hair behaves interactively in the viewport. When the head is moved, the hair responds.

Collision objects can be used to affect the hair, such as this foot leaving a footprint in this hair-generated grass.

Cloth

3ds Max can create simple cloth by using reactor's cloth simulation, but for more-sophisticated applications such as garments, the Cloth system is much more robust. Cloth works much like a clothing design studio. Splines define the shape of the individual fabric panels, which are then stitched together into garments. The process of creating cloth takes several steps. First, splines are used to create the outlines of the cloth sections. These are then turned into surfaces and stitched into garments by using the Garment Maker modifier. The Cloth modifier is added, the fabric is adjusted to fit, and the fabric is simulated for animation.

Creating Patterns from Splines

Creating a garment for a digital character in 3ds Max is similar to creating garments in real life. In real life, a garment is a collection of flat fabric panels that are stitched together. In 3ds Max, the panels are created as splines, which define their outlines. These splines are drawn in the top viewport so they lay flat on the XY-axis. Each panel of the garment is created by using a closed spline. Any holes or darts in the fabric are created as spine outlines within the panel. Patterns can also be imported from various popular pattern-making software packages.

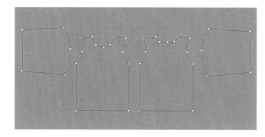

A basic shirt pattern is created by drawing the outlines of the fabric panels as splines.

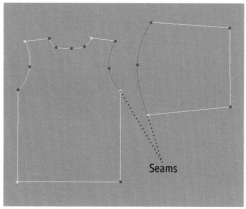

Seams can be defined by creating separate splines along the edges to be seamed.

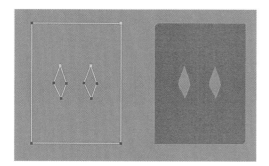

Any closed shapes within another shape will create holes in the fabric, which can also be used as darts to tailor the garment.

Garment Maker

After the pattern is drawn as splines, the Garment Maker modifier is added to the stack, which creates a mesh of all the fabric panels. Garment Maker allows you to specify the mesh of the character and define the key points of the body, such as the arms and neck. After this is done, you can position the panels around the character and define the seams and how the garment will be assembled. The modifier, however, does not sew together the seams; this happens in the Cloth modifier.

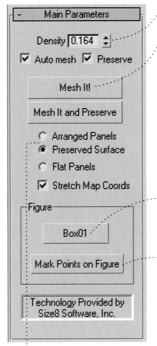

The relative density of the mesh.

When the density value is changed, this recalculates the mesh. Mesh It And Preserve preserves the 3D shape of the mesh in the Cloth modifier so that simulations remain intact.

Chooses the mesh to which the garment will be fitted.

An interactive tool that allows you to define key points on the mesh of the character.

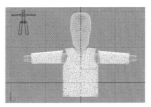

In Mark Points mode, a small figure is created at the top left of the viewport. This figure prompts the user with a red asterisk to select the corresponding location on the mesh. This will make fitting the garment go much more smoothly.

Panels These determine how the panels are passed up the stack to the Cloth modifier.

The Garment Maker Main Parameters rollout

Panels Mode

Panels sub-object mode is where you define each panel and its relative location on the character. Each panel is selected, and then the type of panel is defined in the Panel Position section. After the panels are roughly arranged, they can be seamed.

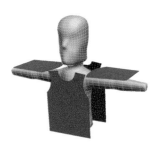

Clothing panels are positioned roughly around the body. Shoulders are placed slightly above the shoulders on the character's mesh so that the garment can "fall" onto the character as it is fitted.

Curvature allows you to curve parts of the garment such as the sleeves. This helps with fitting as well.

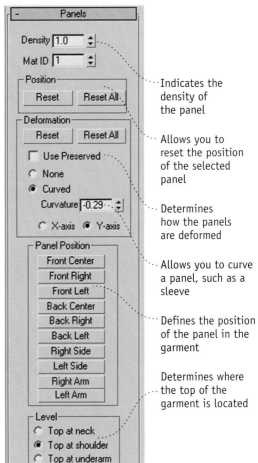

Indicates the density of the panel

Allows you to reset the position of the selected panel

Determines how the panels are deformed

Allows you to curve a panel, such as a sleeve

Defines the position of the panel in the garment

Determines where the top of the garment is located

Seams Mode

Seams sub-object mode allows you to define where the garment is stitched together. Curves on opposite sides of the seam are selected, and the seam is defined by using the Create Seam button. A seam tolerance can be defined to ensure that the seams are of sufficient length to be stitched without bunching.

Creates a seam from the selected curves.

Deletes a selected seam.

Reverses the seam.

Takes two or more curves and makes them a single seam. Useful in attaching the front and back panels of a shirt together so they can be seamed with the sleeve.

Sets the crease angle and crease strength of the seam. A higher crease angle will be more visible.

Indicates the amount of force with which the panels are pulled together at simulation time.

Indicates the maximum difference in length between two edges permitted for a seam. Keeping this value low ensures that the seams will match up without bunching the fabric.

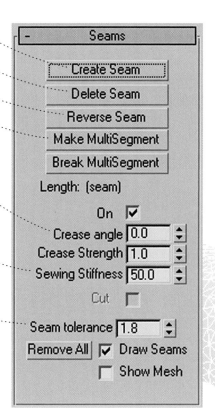

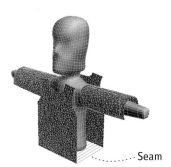

Seams are indicated with graphic stitch lines. The stitching will be pulled together at simulation time.

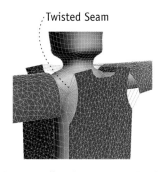

If the curve directions are not lined up, the seam will appear twisted. Reverse Seam will correct this.

Cloth Modifier

After the cloth is meshed and defined in Garment Maker, the Cloth modifier stitches the garment together and performs simulation. This modifier is the heart of the Cloth system, and is where you define cloth and collision objects, create constraints, assign properties, and execute the simulation. The Cloth modifier must be applied to all objects in the cloth simulation. For garments, this means the character's mesh as well as the garment and any other object that may collide with the cloth.

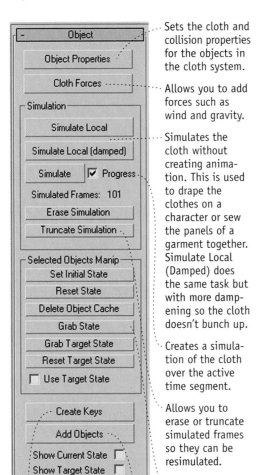

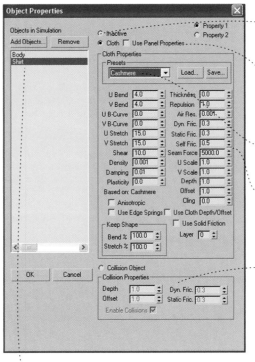

Sets the cloth and collision properties for the objects in the cloth system.

Allows you to add forces such as wind and gravity.

Simulates the cloth without creating animation. This is used to drape the clothes on a character or sew the panels of a garment together. Simulate Local (Damped) does the same task but with more dampening so the cloth doesn't bunch up.

Creates a simulation of the cloth over the active time segment.

Allows you to erase or truncate simulated frames so they can be resimulated.

Provides tools to set, reset, and grab the state of a simulation.

Lets you add objects to the simulation without opening the Object Properties window.

Bakes the simulation to keyframes for rendering. The object is collapsed to an editable mesh, and any deformation is stored as vertex animation.

The Cloth modifier Object rollout provides basic functions for editing cloth properties and creating simulations.

Removes the highlighted object from the simulation.

Allows the cloth properties to be assigned on a panel-by-panel basis.

A pull-down list of common fabric types.

Properties that define the cloth and how it moves, stretches, and deforms.

Properties such as friction for objects that interact with the cloth.

Object List A list of the objects in the current simulation. This includes both cloth and collision objects.

The Object Properties window allows you to define the properties of the objects in the cloth simulation. Objects can be defined as cloth objects, collision objects, or inactive.

Fitting Garments

When using Cloth to simulate clothing, the garment needs to be draped over the character. This is done by using Simulate Local with gravity turned off. This allows the fabric to wrap itself to the mesh of the character. Simulate Local is a simulation, so it can take a little time for the mesh to pull itself together and settle. If the fabric is highly tensile, it may not drape properly. In this case, Simulate Local (Damped) will perform the simulation a little slower and with more damping to allow the fabric to drape more gently. After the fabric is draped, the faces of the cloth can be selected and dragged to position the garment correctly on the character.

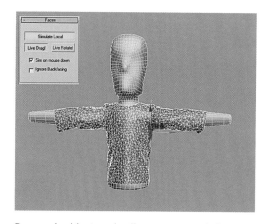

Faces sub-object mode allows you to grab faces of the cloth mesh and move or rotate them during the simulation. When Simulate Local is enabled, you can pull fabric on a character to fit the garment to the mesh.

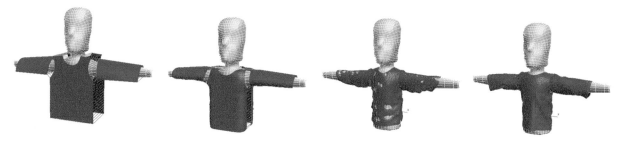

When enabled, Simulate Local pulls the garment together at the seams and drapes the fabric over the character by using a simulation. After the fabric settles, Simulate Local can be disabled.

Adding Forces

Forces can be added to the simulation simply by creating a standard 3ds Max force (Create → Space-Warps → Forces) in the scene. The force is then added to the simulation by pressing the Cloth Forces button. This brings up a window that lists all the forces in the scene; these can then be added to the simulation.

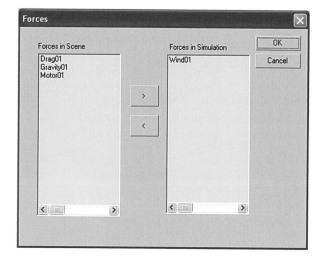

Adding Constraints

Parts of the cloth can be constrained so that it can be attached to other objects. A good example might be a flag attached to a flagpole. These can be set up by using groups, which allows groups of vertices to be affected in different manners. Groups also allow you to change any type of parameter, so you can make areas of the cloth stiffer, for example. Groups can be applied to both the cloth and collision objects in the simulation.

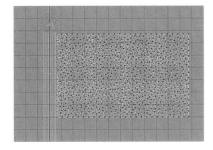

The vertices along the edge of this flag are selected and added to a group. The flagpole is then set as the Node, which attaches the vertices. To attach objects in the simulation, use Sim Node.

The flag is now attached to the flagpole.

The Group sub-object allows you to create groups of vertices to change their properties or constrain them to other objects.

Using Simulation

Simulation calculates the motion of the cloth and how it interacts with the objects in the scene. Simulation is started by pressing the Simulation button in the Object rollout. Once calculated, the simulation can be scrubbed in real time to see how the cloth moves. When the simulation is satisfactory, you can render or use the Create Keys button to create a key for each vertex in the simulation.

The Simulation Parameters rollout specifies general properties of the simulation, such as gravity and start and end frames. These settings apply to all objects in the simulation.

When the character is animated, the cloth will move to match the motion of the character.

Creating Hair

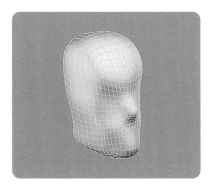

1 Open the file HeadStart.max. This contains a simple head shape to which we can apply hair.

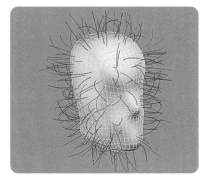

2 Apply the Hair And Fur modifier (Modifiers → Hair And Fur → Hair And Fur (WSM). This creates hair all over the surface.

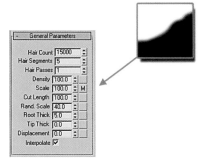

3 We can attenuate the hair by placing a bitmap in the Hair Scale channel. White areas are where the hair is distributed.

4 A quick render shows the results.

5 Open the Styling rollout and click the Style Hair button.

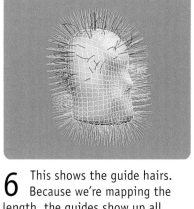

6 This shows the guide hairs. Because we're mapping the length, the guides show up all over the head.

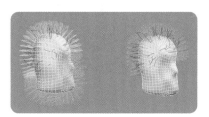

7 We can fix this by selecting the guide hairs and using Attenuate to shorten them.

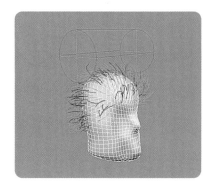

8 Now use the Hair Brush tool to brush the guide hairs into a style.

9 Hair can be selected so it can be brushed in segments. In this case, we're creating a part down the middle by selecting the hairs on one side of the head and brushing them to the side.

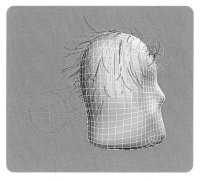

11 The Hair Cut tool allows us to do this. Cut the hair as you desire.

13 Continue the process until you have the desired hairstyle.

10 A quick render shows that the hair is brushed but still needs cutting.

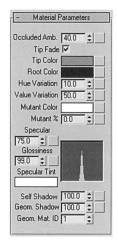

12 Color the hair by using the Material Parameters rollout. Tip Color and Root Color can also be mapped.

About the Companion CD

In this appendix, you'll find information on the following topics:

What you'll find on the CD

System requirements

Using the CD

Troubleshooting

What You'll Find on the CD

This section provides a summary of the software and other goodies you'll find on the CD. If you need help installing the items provided on the CD, refer to the installation instructions in the "Using the CD" section of this appendix.

Tutorial Files

All the .max files provided in this book for completing the tutorials are located in the Tutorials Files directory on the CD and work with Windows 2000, NT, XP, and Vista.

3ds Max Trial Version

The Autodesk 3ds Max 30-day trial provides free access to the software for noncommercial use. Animation and 3D graphics students, industry professionals, or anyone interested in breaking into the world of computer graphics (CG) now has the opportunity to explore all aspects of the 3ds Max software. This product is subject to the terms and conditions of the end-user license agreement that accompanies the software.

Autodesk and 3ds Max are registered trademarks of Autodesk, Inc., in the United States and other countries.

For more information and software updates, visit www.autodesk.com/3dsmax.

System Requirements

Make sure that your computer meets the minimum system requirements shown here. If your computer doesn't match up to most of these requirements, you may have problems using the software and files on the companion CD. For the latest information, please refer to the ReadMe file located at the root of the CD-ROM.

At a minimum, for the 32-bit version of 3ds Max, you'll need a laptop or desktop PC running Windows 2000 Pro or XP Professional with at least 512MB of RAM, 500MB of swap space, and an Intel Pentium IV or AMD Athlon XP or higher processor. You'll also need a hardware-accelerated OpenGL or Direct3D video card. The requirements for the 64-bit version are higher.

See the Autodesk website for the most up-to-date requirements:

`http://usa.autodesk.com/adsk/servlet/index?siteID=123112&id=5659453.`

Using the CD

To install the items from the CD to your hard disk, follow these steps:

1. Insert the CD into your computer's CD-ROM drive. The license agreement appears.

> Windows users: The interface won't launch if you have autorun disabled. In that case, click Start → Run (for Windows Vista, Start → All Programs → Accessories → Run). In the dialog box that appears, type **D:\Start.exe**. (Replace *D* with the proper letter if your CD drive uses a different letter. If you don't know the letter, see how your CD drive is listed under My Computer.) Click OK.

2. Read through the license agreement, and then click the Accept button if you want to use the CD.

The CD interface appears. The interface allows you to access the content with just one or two clicks.

Troubleshooting

Wiley has attempted to provide programs that work on most computers with the minimum system requirements. Alas, your computer may differ, and some programs may not work properly for some reason.

The two likeliest problems are that you don't have enough memory (RAM) for the programs you want to use, or you have other programs running that are affecting installation or running of a program. If you get an error message such as "Not enough memory" or "Setup cannot continue," try one or more of the following suggestions and then try using the software again:

Turn off any antivirus software running on your computer. Installation programs sometimes mimic virus activity and may make your computer incorrectly believe that it's being infected by a virus.

Close all running programs. The more programs you have running, the less memory is available to other programs. Installation programs typically update files and programs; so if you keep other programs running, installation may not work properly.

Have your local computer store add more RAM to your computer. This is, admittedly, a drastic and somewhat expensive step. However, adding more memory can really help the speed of your computer and allow more programs to run at the same time.

Customer Care

If you have trouble with the book's companion CD-ROM, please call the Wiley Product Technical Support phone number at (800) 762-2974. Outside the United States, call (001)-317-572-3994. You can also contact Wiley Product Technical Support at `http://sybex.custhelp.com`. John Wiley & Sons will provide technical support only for installation and other general quality-control items. For technical support on the applications themselves, consult the program's vendor or author.

To place additional orders or to request information about other Wiley products, please call (877) 762-2974.

Index

Wiley Publishing, Inc.
End-User License Agreement

READ THIS. You should carefully read these terms and conditions before opening the software packet(s) included with this book "Book". This is a license agreement "Agreement" between you and Wiley Publishing, Inc. "WPI". By opening the accompanying software packet(s), you acknowledge that you have read and accept the following terms and conditions. If you do not agree and do not want to be bound by such terms and conditions, promptly return the Book and the unopened software packet(s) to the place you obtained them for a full refund.

1. **License Grant.** WPI grants to you (either an individual or entity) a nonexclusive license to use one copy of the enclosed software program(s) (collectively, the "Software") solely for your own personal or business purposes on a single computer (whether a standard computer or a workstation component of a multi-user network). The Software is in use on a computer when it is loaded into temporary memory (RAM) or installed into permanent memory (hard disk, CD-ROM, or other storage device). WPI reserves all rights not expressly granted herein.

2. **Ownership.** WPI is the owner of all right, title, and interest, including copyright, in and to the compilation of the Software recorded on the physical packet included with this Book "Software Media". Copyright to the individual programs recorded on the Software Media is owned by the author or other authorized copyright owner of each program. Ownership of the Software and all proprietary rights relating thereto remain with WPI and its licensers.

3. **Restrictions on Use and Transfer.**

   (a) You may only (i) make one copy of the Software for backup or archival purposes, or (ii) transfer the Software to a single hard disk, provided that you keep the original for backup or archival purposes. You may not (i) rent or lease the Software, (ii) copy or reproduce the Software through a LAN or other network system or through any computer subscriber system or bulletin-board system, or (iii) modify, adapt, or create derivative works based on the Software.

   (b) You may not reverse engineer, decompile, or disassemble the Software. You may transfer the Software and user documentation on a permanent basis, provided that the transferee agrees to accept the terms and conditions of this Agreement and you retain no copies. If the Software is an update or has been updated, any transfer must include the most recent update and all prior versions.

4. **Restrictions on Use of Individual Programs.** You must follow the individual requirements and restrictions detailed for each individual program in the "About the CD" appendix of this Book or on the Software Media. These limitations are also contained in the individual license agreements recorded on the Software Media. These limitations may include a requirement that after using the program for a specified period of time, the user must pay a registration fee or discontinue use. By opening the Software packet(s), you agree to abide by the licenses and restrictions for these individual programs that are detailed in the "About the CD" appendix and/or on the Software Media. None of the material on this Software Media or listed in this Book may ever be redistributed, in original or modified form, for commercial purposes.

5. **Limited Warranty.**

   (a) WPI warrants that the Software and Software Media are free from defects in materials and workmanship under normal use for a period of sixty (60) days from the date of purchase of this Book. If WPI receives notification within the warranty period of defects in materials or workmanship, WPI will replace the defective Software Media.

   (b) WPI AND THE AUTHOR(S) OF THE BOOK DISCLAIM ALL OTHER WARRANTIES, EXPRESS OR IMPLIED, INCLUDING WITHOUT LIMITATION IMPLIED WARRANTIES OF MERCHANTABILITY AND FITNESS FOR A PARTICULAR PURPOSE, WITH RESPECT TO THE SOFTWARE, THE PROGRAMS, THE SOURCE CODE CONTAINED THEREIN, AND/OR THE TECHNIQUES DESCRIBED IN THIS BOOK. WPI DOES NOT WARRANT THAT THE FUNCTIONS CONTAINED IN THE SOFTWARE WILL MEET YOUR REQUIREMENTS OR THAT THE OPERATION OF THE SOFTWARE WILL BE ERROR FREE.

   (c) This limited warranty gives you specific legal rights, and you may have other rights that vary from jurisdiction to jurisdiction.

6. **Remedies.**

   (a) WPI's entire liability and your exclusive remedy for defects in materials and workmanship shall be limited to replacement of the Software Media, which may be returned to WPI with a copy of your receipt at the following address: Software Media Fulfillment Department, Attn.: *3ds Max at a Glance*, Wiley Publishing, Inc., 10475 Crosspoint Blvd., Indianapolis, IN 46256, or call 1-800-762-2974. Please allow four to six weeks for delivery. This Limited Warranty is void if failure of the Software Media has resulted from accident, abuse, or misapplication. Any replacement Software Media will be warranted for the remainder of the original warranty period or thirty (30) days, whichever is longer.

   (b) In no event shall WPI or the author be liable for any damages whatsoever (including without limitation damages for loss of business profits, business interruption, loss of business information, or any other pecuniary loss) arising from the use of or inability to use the Book or the Software, even if WPI has been advised of the possibility of such damages.

   (c) Because some jurisdictions do not allow the exclusion or limitation of liability for consequential or incidental damages, the above limitation or exclusion may not apply to you.

7. **U.S. Government Restricted Rights.** Use, duplication, or disclosure of the Software for or on behalf of the United States of America, its agencies and/or instrumentalities "U.S. Government" is subject to restrictions as stated in paragraph (c)(1)(ii) of the Rights in Technical Data and Computer Software clause of DFARS 252.227-7013, or subparagraphs (c) (1) and (2) of the Commercial Computer Software - Restricted Rights clause at FAR 52.227-19, and in similar clauses in the NASA FAR supplement, as applicable.

8. **General.** This Agreement constitutes the entire understanding of the parties and revokes and supersedes all prior agreements, oral or written, between them and may not be modified or amended except in a writing signed by both parties hereto that specifically refers to this Agreement. This Agreement shall take precedence over any other documents that may be in conflict herewith. If any one or more provisions contained in this Agreement are held by any court or tribunal to be invalid, illegal, or otherwise unenforceable, each and every other provision shall remain in full force and effect.